Toward Resili‹

Praise for this book...

"This guide is an easy-to-use resource that provides guidance for NGO staff and partners alike to tackle the issues of disasters and climate change. Not only does it provide 10 common sense principles for integrating disaster risk reduction and climate change adaptation in practice, it highlights the needs of vulnerable populations including children, so that they can be part of the process of building disaster and climate resilience."

Dr Nick Hall
Head of DRR and CCA, Save the Children

"For vulnerable communities in the Pacific that are already experiencing the profound impacts of disasters and climate change, this guide is a fantastic resource. Not only does it recognize the importance of involving local people to build on their existing strengths to prepare for disasters and adapt to climate change, it provides practical guidance for identifying high-risk groups (including children, young people, women, older people, and those with disabilities) and how to work with them effectively. Congratulations on a great resource."

Maria Tiimon,
Pacific Outreach Officer, Pacific Calling Partnership, Edmund Rice Centre

"While others still find it difficult to climb out of their silos and blink in the sunlight, the civil society organisations and INGOs that use these rigorously produced 'good enough' guidelines will come much, much closer to providing a fully integrated approach to disaster risk, climate change and livelihood enhancement. Once again ECB has produced a winner!"

Dr Ben Wisner,
Aon Benfield UCL Hazard Research Centre, University College London

Toward Resilience

A Guide to Disaster Risk Reduction and Climate Change Adaptation

Marilise Turnbull, Charlotte L. Sterrett,
Amy Hilleboe

Practical Action Publishing Ltd
The Schumacher Centre
Bourton on Dunsmore, Rugby,
Warwickshire CV23 9QZ, UK
www.practicalactionpublishing.org

ISBN 978-1-85339-786-8 Paperback
ISBN 978-1-78044-786-5 Ebook
ISBN 978-1-78044-002-6 Library Ebook

A catalogue record for this book is available from the British Library.

The authors have asserted their rights under the Copyright Designs and Patents Act 1988 to be identified as authors of this work.

Since 1974, Practical Action Publishing (formerly Intermediate Technology Publications and ITDG Publishing) has published and disseminated books and information in support of international development work throughout the world. Practical Action Publishing is a trading name of Practical Action Publishing Ltd (Company Reg. No. 1159018), the wholly owned publishing company of Practical Action. Practical Action Publishing trades only in support of its parent charity objectives and any profits are covenanted back to Practical Action (Charity Reg. No. 247257, Group VAT Registration No. 880 9924 76).

Cover photo: Erin Gray/Mercy Corps
Front cover design: Solveig Marina Bang
Indexed by Liz Fawcett
Typeset by Wildfire Press Limited
Printed by Hobbs the Printer, UK.

Contents

Terms that are in the glossary are marked with a superscript 'G'.

INTRODUCTION

Purpose of the guide

Toward Resilience: A Guide to Disaster Risk Reduction and Climate Change Adaptation is an introductory resource for staff of development and humanitarian organizations working with people whose lives and rights are threatened by disasters and climate change.

The guide provides essential introductory information, principles of effective practice, guidelines for action in a range of sectors and settings, case studies and links to useful tools and resources, for the application of an integrated, rights-based approach to disaster risk reduction and climate change adaptation.

The guide is also a useful resource for other stakeholders, including staff from local, district and national government offices, the United Nations, donors, as well as social and natural scientists.

Toward Resilience is not intended to replace individual organizations' policies or guidelines for disaster risk reduction and climate change adaptation; rather, it seeks to foster complementary practices and coordination between multiple actors working towards a common goal.

Contents and structure of the guide

Chapter 1 explains the evolution of disaster risk reduction and climate change adaptation and the rationale for an integrated approach to building resilience. It presents 10 principles for effective programming and advocacy, based on extensive research and practice.

Chapter 2 describes the impacts of disaster and climate change risk on children, women and men, and high-risk populations: people living with disabilities, people living with chronic diseases, older people and indigenous peoples. It provides a checklist for promoting the participation of key groups in risk analysis and actions to build resilience.

Chapter 3 explains program cycle management for interventions to reduce disaster and climate change risk. It includes key issues and steps to follow at each stage of the program cycle, and guidance for knowledge generation and management throughout.

Chapter 4 highlights the need to incorporate measures to reduce disaster and climate change risk in the main sectors of developmental and humanitarian intervention: food security; livelihoods; natural resource management; water, sanitation and hygiene (WASH); education; health; and protection. It provides guidance on how to apply the principles for effective programming and advocacy to build resilience in each sector.

Chapter 5 explains the value of incorporating measures to reduce disaster and climate change risk in interventions in four challenging contexts for development and humanitarian work: conflict settings; early recovery; urban environments; and slow-onset disasters. It provides guidance on how to apply the principles for effective programming and advocacy to build resilience in each context.

Chapter 6 describes the importance of governance and advocacy for the creation of an enabling environment for resilience-building. It provides guidance on how to apply the principles for effective interventions in these closely-related areas of work.

Each of the above chapters includes case studies from practitioners' experiences to illustrate examples of program activities, good practices and lessons learned.

Finally, a tools and resources section guides practitioners to relevant material to use according to their specific needs.

Toward Resilience: A Guide to Disaster Risk Reduction and Climate Change Adaptation is available in a handbook form, and at www.ecbproject.org

How the guide was developed

Toward Resilience: A Guide to Disaster Risk Reduction and Climate Change Adaptation is the product of three years of collaboration and lesson-sharing between ECB Project agencies working with populations at risk of disasters and the impacts of climate change.

Multi-agency teams identified a clear need for a resource that would combine guidance on programming and advocacy for disaster risk reduction and climate change adaptation. The ECB Project agencies engaged in a process of consultation and experience-sharing involving over 160 staff working on development and humanitarian programs in 12 countries.

Simultaneously, studies by other relevant actors, donors and alliances—including the UNISDR, the Intergovernmental Panel on Climate Change (IPCC), the United Nations Framework Convention on Climate Change (UNFCCC), the British Government's Department for International Development (DFID), and ECHO—in the fields of disaster risk reduction, climate change adaptation and 'resilience-building' were collected and analyzed, and have informed the guide's development.

Toward Resilience: A Guide to Disaster Risk Reduction and Climate Change Adaptation was released on the International Day for Disaster Reduction, 2012.

UNDERSTANDING
DISASTER RISK REDUCTION AND CLIMATE CHANGE ADAPTATION

Chapter 1 is designed to help development and humanitarian practitioners understand the basic concepts of disaster risk reduction[G] and climate change adaptation[G], as well as the benefits and key elements of an integrated approach to building resilience[G] to disaster and climate change risk. It includes:

- *Explanations* of:
    - The challenges posed by disasters and climate change;
    - The evolution of disaster risk reduction and climate change adaptation as concepts and in practice;
    - The rationale for an integrated approach to disaster risk reduction and climate change adaptation.
- 10 *principles* for integrated disaster risk reduction and climate change adaptation.
- *Answers* to frequently asked questions.

1.1 Disaster and climate change risk concepts

Disaster risk

Development and humanitarian practitioners share a common goal: the empowerment of women, men and children to enjoy their human rights, and the ongoing protection[G] of those rights. Development strategies and humanitarian responses need, therefore, to incorporate measures to reduce the main risks to achieving this goal.

But the impacts of disasters[G] continue to be a major obstacle to this. Recorded disasters alone from 2001 to 2010 affected, on average, 232 million people per year, killed 106 million others, and caused US$108 billion in economic damages[1]. In addition, countless small-scale, unreported disasters put a cumulative strain on health, lives and livelihoods[G].

It is now widely accepted that disasters are not unavoidable interruptions to development, to be dealt with solely through rapid delivery of emergency relief, but are the result of unmanaged risks[G] within the development process itself. They are created when a hazard[G], such as a flood or earthquake, occurs where people, assets and systems are exposed and vulnerable to its effects.

Conversely, disaster risk can be significantly reduced through strategies that seek to decrease vulnerability[G] and exposure[G] to hazards within wider efforts to address poverty and inequality. Humanitarian responses to disasters and other crises can be designed and implemented in ways that protect the affected people's right to life and other basic rights in the short and longer term. This approach is known as disaster risk reduction.

Box 1.1: Definitions of disasters and disaster risk

Disasters[G] are recognized within the humanitarian and development sectors as situations that involve a major and widespread disruption to life in a community or society, from which most people are not able to recover without assistance from others, often from outside that community or society. They typically involve widespread loss of life, infrastructure and other assets, and impact on people's wellbeing, security, health and livelihoods. Some disaster impacts are immediate and others can be exacerbated by the way people react to the situation and attempt to recover from it.

Disaster risk[G] is the potential disaster losses—in lives, health status, livelihoods, assets and services—that could occur to a particular community or a society over a specified time period.

Disaster risk reduction

Disaster risk reduction is defined as: *"The concept and practice of reducing disaster risks through systematic efforts to analyze and manage the causal factors of disasters, including through reduced exposure to hazards, lessened vulnerability of people and property, wise management of land and the environment, and improved preparedness for adverse events."*[2]

People around the world constantly seek ways to reduce disaster risks. Some combine diverse livelihood strategies, such as fishing, farming and selling manual labor, to reduce their vulnerability to losses in one area; some use social networks to obtain information about good pasture, or impending hazards, such as swollen rivers, and plan their actions accordingly. But in many cases poverty and marginalization restrict their effectiveness and options, and rural-to-urban migration exposes them to unfamiliar situations in which they lack the knowledge and means to manage new risks.

Today, there is increasing awareness that states—within their obligation to respect, fulfill and protect human rights—have primary responsibility for reducing disaster risk, and that the international community has a duty to provide support and create an enabling environment for this obligation to be met. By signing the Hyogo Framework for Action (HFA) at the World Conference on Disaster Reduction in 2005, 168 governments and all leading development and humanitarian actors committed to a 10 year multi-stakeholder and multi-sectoral plan to invest in disaster risk reduction as a means to building disaster-resilient societies.

Since the HFA was agreed, many governments have introduced legislative and policy frameworks for disaster risk reduction, established early warning systems[G] and increased their level of preparedness[G] to respond to disasters. However, the goals of the HFA are still far from being achieved, particularly in terms of addressing the causes of risk and ensuring full participation of at-risk populations in risk assessments, planning processes and programs. A massive effort is needed to bring about change at the heart of each country's 'development system' through the involvement of all sectors and all stakeholders[G]—from local to national—in disaster risk reduction.

Box 1.2: Hyogo Framework for Action

The Hyogo Framework for Action has five priorities for action:

1. Prioritizing disaster risk reduction by providing high-profile leadership, establishing relevant policies and programs, and allocating resources to implement them.

2. Identifying, assessing and monitoring disaster risks and improving early warning systems.

3. Creating awareness at all levels of society about risk and providing information about how to reduce it.

4. Reducing social, economic and environmental vulnerabilities and those related to land use through improved development planning and post-disaster reconstruction by all sectors.

5. Strengthening disaster preparedness for effective response at all levels.

Source: UNISDR (2005) Hyogo Framework for Action 2005-2015: Building the Resilience of Nations and Communities to Disasters.

Climate change risk

As scientific knowledge of global climate change[G] increases and its impacts are experienced around the world, there is a clear need for a broader approach to reducing risks.

> **Box 1.3: Definition of climate change**
>
> Various definitions of climate change exist, but the working definition used in the guide defines climate change as a change in the average pattern of weather over a long period of time, typically decades or longer.[3]

Current global climate change is understood to be the result of human activities since the Industrial Revolution—such as the burning of fossil fuels[G] and land-use change[G] (for example, deforestation[G])—resulting in a significant increase in greenhouse gases[G] such as carbon dioxide.[4] While greenhouse gases are a natural part of the Earth's atmosphere and serve to maintain temperatures to support life, excessive emission of these is causing more heat to be trapped in the atmosphere, leading to rising temperatures.[5]

Projected changes in the climate include temperature increases on land and at sea, sea-level rise, melting of glaciers and ice caps, and changing and irregular rainfall patterns. These changes affect almost every aspect of human life and the ecosystems on which it depends.

Climate change will result in increases in the frequency and intensity of extreme weather events, as well as significant impacts from more gradual changes[G].[6] The nature, extent and duration of climate change effects on regions vary. Efforts to reduce the impacts of climate change are known as climate change adaptation.

Climate change adaptation

Climate change adaptation is a practice covering actions by a range of actors to manage and reduce the risks associated with changes in the climate. Varying technical and scientific definitions exist to best serve the purposes of different actors involved in the climate change sphere. For the purposes of this guide the following simplified working definition of climate change adaptation is used:[7]

a) Adapting development to gradual changes in average temperature, sea-level and precipitation; and,

b) Reducing and managing the risks associated with more frequent, severe and unpredictable extreme weather events.

People have always adapted to climate variability[G] through a variety of means including, for example, planting late-transplant rice or switching to other, faster-growing crops. However climate change is pushing at-risk populations beyond their capacity[G] to cope and adapt to the changes they have traditionally dealt with, as well as making more people vulnerable due to their increased sensitivity and exposure to climate change impacts.

Governments and institutions are coming to realize that security, poverty reduction and prosperity will depend on the integration of climate change adaptation strategies in all sectors, and their implementation at all levels. Development and humanitarian practitioners also have an important role to play in terms of advocating for the rights of the women, men and children at greatest risk to be prioritized, and incorporating climate change adaptation strategies into their own programs.

As an approach, climate change adaptation is a dynamic process and not an end state, given the uncertainty in climate change impacts and the need to support at-risk populations to: address current hazards, increased variability and emerging trends; manage risk and uncertainty; and build their capacity to adapt.[8]

Table 1.1: Examples of climate-related hazards and effects, and adaptation activities*		
Hazard or effect	Impact	Adaptation activity examples
Hazard— Intense rainfall	• Increased frequency/ severity of floods • Damage to housing, infrastructure and livelihoods	• Improvement of drainage in rural and urban areas • Protection/retrofitting of water-supply and sanitation systems to prevent damage and contamination • Promotion of raised-bed agriculture[G] • (Re-)location of critical infrastructure and housing away from flood-prone areas
Hazard— Storm	• Damage to housing, infrastructure and livelihoods	• Retrofitting/construction of infrastructure and housing using storm-resilient designs and materials • Introduction/strengthening of early warning systems to alert exposed populations • Designation of 'safe places' for shelter and storage during storms
Effect— Temperature increase	• Heat stress on crops • Increased crop water demand and/ or reduced water availability	• Increased accessibility to drought-tolerant crop varieties • Promotion of techniques to increase organic content of soil (for greater water retention) • Promotion of agroforestry practices and/ or conservation agriculture practices which result in improved soil microclimate and reduced evapo-transpiration
Effect— Sea-level rise	• Saline intrusion • Coastal erosion • Increased frequency/ severity of storm surges[G]	• Identification of alternative, sustainable water sources for human consumption and livelihood use • Increased accessibility to saline-tolerant crop varieties • Strengthened sea defenses (natural—such as mangroves—and engineered)

Table 1.1: Examples of climate-related hazards and effects, and adaptation activities*		
Hazard or effect	Impact	Adaptation activity examples
Effect— Changed seasonality	• Farmers uncertain about when to cultivate, sow and harvest	• Increased productivity of existing livelihood activities • Provision of user-appropriate, accessible and reliable climate and weather forecasts • Promotion of crop diversification and mixing. • Facilitation of resources for livelihoods diversification

* The examples listed are not exhaustive. When designing adaptation options, the particular context should be taken into account.

Box 1.4: The changing face of disaster risk

Climate change is altering the face of disaster risk, not only through increased weather-related risks and sea-level and temperature rises, but also through increases in societal vulnerabilities, for example, from stresses on water availability, agriculture and ecosystems. Disaster risk reduction and climate change adaptation share a common space of concern: reducing the vulnerability of communities and achieving sustainable development.

1.2   Constructing an integrated approach to disaster risk reduction and climate change adaptation

Increasingly, development and humanitarian practitioners are discovering the need for, and advantages of, using an approach that integrates concepts and practices from both disaster risk reduction and climate change adaptation, as explained below:

Common concerns

There is significant convergence between the problems that disaster risk reduction and climate change adaptation seek to address. As shown in Figure 1.1, populations already exposed to climate-related hazards^G and effects will be at greater risk due to a projected increase in the frequency and/or intensity of those hazards and effects as a result of global climate change.

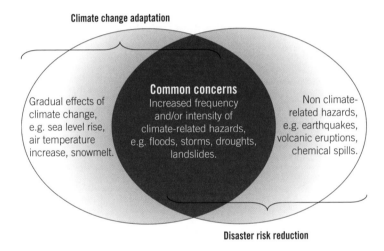

Figure 1.1: Common concerns of climate change adaptation and disaster risk reduction

Furthermore, populations exposed to hazards may experience stresses^G due to longer-term changes in the climate—such as changes in seasonality, unpredictable rainfall, and sea-level rise—that affect their livelihoods and health, making them more vulnerable to all types of shocks^G, events and further changes.[9]

A common conceptual understanding of risk

Disaster risk reduction and climate change adaptation also share a common conceptual understanding of the components of risk and the processes of building resilience. The two approaches regard risk as the product of exposure and vulnerability, either to hazard(s) or effect(s) of climate change, or both. The greater the vulnerability, exposure and magnitude or likelihood of the hazard/climate change effect, the greater the risk.

Both exposure and vulnerability are compounded by other societal and environmental trends, for example, urbanization, environmental degradation^G, and the globalization of markets.

Thus, to reduce disaster and climate change risk, exposure needs to be minimized, vulnerability reduced, and capacities for resilience strengthened in ways that address both disaster and climate change risk simultaneously, neither approach compromising the other. This is a dynamic process requiring continual effort across economic, social, cultural, environmental, institutional and political spheres to move from vulnerability to resilience.

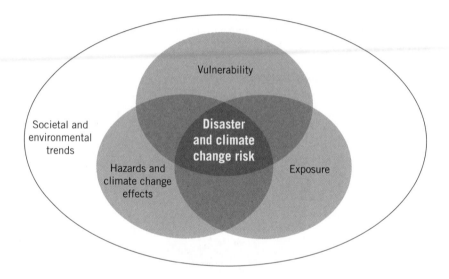

Figure 1.2: Disaster and climate change risk

Box 1.5: Key terms used in *Toward Resilience*

- **Hazards** are potentially harmful natural phenomena or human activities that, when they occur, may cause loss of life, injury or other health impacts, property damage, loss of livelihoods and services, social and economic disruption, and environmental damage. Hazards include: droughts, floods, earthquakes, volcanic eruptions, epidemics, windstorms, heavy precipitation, chemical spills, conflict^G, and others.

- **Climate change effects** are changes in the climate as a result of excessive emission of greenhouse gas. Effects include temperature increases on land and at sea; rises in sea-level; the melting of glaciers and ice caps; and changing and irregular rainfall patterns. As a result of the effects of climate change, existing climate-related hazards such as droughts, floods and windstorms are projected to increase in frequency and/or intensity. The planet is locked into some degree of climate change, but technological and political decisions to reduce it can still be taken.

Box 1.5: Key terms used in *Toward Resilience* (cont.)

- **Exposure** refers to the people, property, livelihood assets, systems, and other elements present in areas likely to be affected by hazards and/or effects of climate change.

- **Vulnerability** is the set of characteristics and circumstances of an individual, household, population group, system or asset that make it susceptible (or sensitive, in the case of ecosystems) to the damaging effects of a hazard and/or effects of climate change. These characteristics and circumstances can be physical, institutional, political, cultural, social, environmental, economic and human.

- **Resilience** refers to the capacity^G of an individual, household, population group or system to anticipate, absorb, and recover from hazards and/or effects of climate change and other shocks and stresses without compromising (and potentially enhancing) long-term prospects.[10] Resilience is not a fixed end state, but is a dynamic set of conditions and processes. The factors that influence resilience are shown in Figure 1.3.

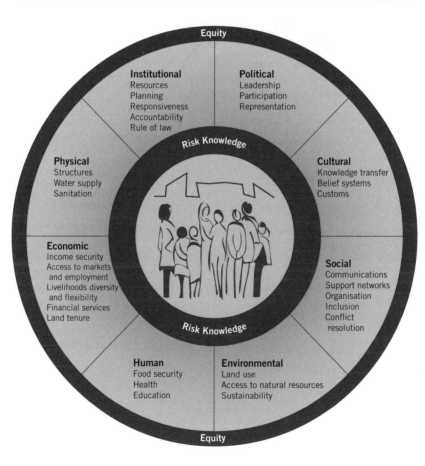

Figure 1.3: Factors influencing resilience

Similarity of impacts

The impacts of disasters[G] and effects of climate change have similar consequences for people's lives and the extent to which they are able to realize and enjoy their rights, as shown in Figure 1.4. Disasters and the shocks and stresses caused by effects of climate change can cause significant losses which, in turn, increase vulnerability, resulting in a downward trend of impoverishment and denial of rights.

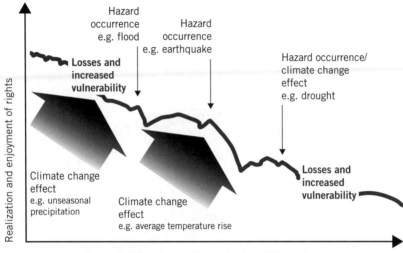

Figure 1.4: Similarity of impacts of disasters and other effects of climate change

Disaster risk reduction and climate change adaptation share a goal: both approaches seek to strengthen people's and societies' capacity for resilience so that their own efforts and those of development interventions may lead to full realization and enjoyment of their rights.

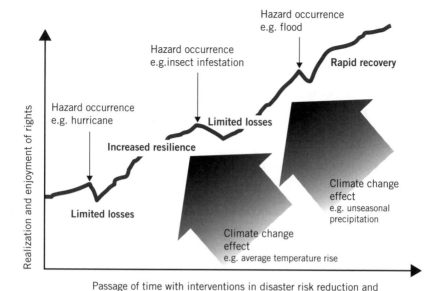

Figure 1.5: Similarity of objectives of disaster risk reduction and climate change adaptation

1.3   Principles of an integrated approach to disaster risk reduction and climate change adaptation

As global commitment to and investment in disaster risk reduction has grown, so has practitioners' and policy-makers' knowledge of good practice, enabling factors, and barriers to success. Meanwhile, innovative action-research in the field of climate change adaptation is rapidly producing valuable indicators of the fundamental elements for effective adaptation programming. Most recently, interest among development and humanitarian actors in improving understanding of how to generate greater resilience to shocks and stresses, including hazards and the effects of climate change, is resulting in constructive debate. There is significant convergence in the lessons, recommendations and challenges emerging from each of these spheres of activity, and a growing consensus on the need for an integrated approach.

The following **10 principles for an integrated approach to disaster risk reduction and climate change adaptation** are drawn from this increasing body of knowledge.[11] Together, these principles provide development and humanitarian practitioners with a set of criteria for building disaster and climate resilience that is applicable across the program cycle in multiple sectors and varied contexts.

1. **Increase understanding of the hazard and climate change context**: An understanding of past trends, present experiences and future projections of hazard occurrence, climate variability and the range of effects of climate change on the area and population concerned should underpin any decisions or actions to build disaster and climate resilience. It should include mapping at different scales, to allow for regional and local hazards and effects of climate change. The risk analysis process itself should increase understanding among all stakeholders[G], both as a result of its participatory nature, and through sharing of the results.

2. **Increase understanding of exposure, vulnerability and capacity**: An assessment of the vulnerabilities and capacities of the population, systems and resources should be the foundation for decisions on the location, target populations (including understanding differential vulnerability), objectives and approach of measures to build disaster and climate resilience. It should include analysis of the projected effects of climate change as well as of those currently observed. The assessment should also increase understanding among all stakeholders of the causes of exposure, vulnerability and capacity, both as a result of a participatory process, and through sharing of the results.

3. **Recognize rights and responsibilities**: Disaster risk reduction and climate change adaptation should be regarded among the responsibilities of states and governments as duty-bearers for the realization and enjoyment of human rights. Governance[G] systems and the political environment should enable people at risk or affected by disasters and climate change to demand accountability for their decisions, actions and omissions. The role of other stakeholders, including NGOs, should be complementary to, and enabling of, the relationship between duty-bearers and right-holders.

4. **Strengthen participation of, and action by, the population at risk**: All people at risk have the right to participate in decisions that affect their lives. Their first-hand knowledge of the issues affecting them is critical to ensuring that analysis and subsequent actions are based on empirical evidence. In addition, the sustainability of resilience-building strategies depends on their ownership and agency. Therefore all decision-making processes and actions should directly involve the population at risk ensuring that women, men and children, as well as high-risk groups, are included.

5. **Promote systemic engagement and change**: As there are multiple causes and drivers of vulnerability and exposure to hazards and the effects of climate change, strategies to build disaster and climate resilience should engage all sectors of society and government. The goal of multi-sectoral and multi-stakeholder engagement should be to make building disaster and climate resilience central to development planning. The commitment of all actors to this goal should be reflected in their respective policies, plans and budgets.

6. **Foster synergy between multiple levels**: The importance of an enabling political environment is critical to actions taken at the household, community and local levels. Similarly, the impact of a policy or law depends on its implementation by different levels of government and its relevance to the population at risk. Decisions and actions taken at each level should be mutually informative and facilitate the development of a coherent and coordinated approach.

7. **Draw on and build diverse sources of knowledge**: Analysis of disaster and climate change risk should seek to complement local and traditional knowledge with the results of scientific research in order to continue to co-generate new knowledge. Measures to build disaster and climate resilience should promote replication of effective practices, encourage autonomous innovation and introduce, where appropriate, external technology to help address new or magnified challenges. Strategies and programs should be monitored and evaluated to ensure that learning is captured and made available to others.

8. **Instill flexibility and responsiveness**: As the effects and impacts of climate change remain uncertain, particularly on a local scale, and many dynamic processes (such as urbanization and environmental degradation^G) influence exposure and vulnerability, analysis of disaster and climate change risk should be responsive to emerging knowledge. Similarly, strategies and programs to build disaster and climate resilience should be flexible, to accommodate new inputs.

9. **Address different timescales**: Analysis, strategies and programs should address current, identified risks and likely future scenarios. Preparing for the occurrence of known hazards should not be neglected in favor of building capacities to adapt to medium- and long-term effects of climate change, and other, potentially unknown shocks or stresses. Resource allocation and activities should be planned accordingly.

10. **Do no harm**: Processes to define strategies and programs to build disaster and climate resilience should always incorporate an assessment of their potential negative impacts, including their contribution to conflict and effects on the environment. In cases where potential harm is identified, measures to substantially reduce or remove them should be built into the strategy and program design. To avoid creating a false sense of security, or promoting mal-adaptation^G, programs should always be based on a multi-hazard, multi-effect assessment.

Chapters 3 to 6 of this guide indicate how to apply an integrated approach to disaster risk reduction and climate change adaptation across the program cycle, in different sectoral interventions, and in varied settings.

CASE STUDY: ADAPTING TO INCREASING CLIMATE CHANGE VULNERABILITY IN CENTRAL COASTAL PROVINCES OF VIETNAM[12]

Vietnam, World Vision International

Along Vietnam's 3,000km long coastline and extensive low-lying river deltas, sea-level rise and saltwater inundation caused by climate change, are significant long-term threats to the production of rice and aquaculture on which people's livelihoods depend.[13] More immediate threats are typhoons, which are increasing in severity, and floods, that are becoming more frequent.

In 2005, World Vision started working in the central coastal province of Quang Ngai, where communities have been experiencing significant difficulties in recovering from disasters. To promote local adaptive capacity, a project focused on improving the range of locally available assets to build community resilience to the impact of disasters and climate extremes. Forty-three small- and medium-sized infrastructure facilities were constructed in 37 hamlets including raising and concreting earth roads—to facilitate travel in the wet season—and schoolyards were raised so that children could avoid contact with contaminated water. More than 1,000 households from 49 hamlets also received loans to improve the construction of their homes. The project also focused on creating alternative income-generation opportunities for families so that they were no longer reliant on growing a single crop, with 2,583 households receiving support for additional income-generation activities such as growing bamboo or selling household products in order to diversify away from rice cultivation and aquaculture.

School-based programs ensured that children had the knowledge and information to enable them to make sound judgments and protect themselves in the event of a disaster. The Red Cross provided wireless communication systems and broadcast stations to inform communities about disaster preparedness. The project also contributed to flexible forward-thinking decision making and governance by creating household and hamlet disaster risk reduction plans (DRRPs), and **fostered synergy between multiple levels** by integrating these into the community, district and provincial level plans. To **strengthen participation of, and action by, the population at risk**, more than 100 hamlet facilitators and 10 rescue teams were established and trained in natural disaster mitigation and first aid. In turn, they helped more than 7,000 households develop their own disaster risk reduction plans, as well as 10 commune and 50 hamlet DRRPs, which were all integrated into existing plans at the district and national level. The wellbeing of children was directly improved through school-based programs on disaster preparedness reaching 500 teachers and 20,000 students.

Lessons learned included: (a) Working within the existing government structure to integrate local level plans is key to fostering support from the government and facilitating support and resources for local level initiatives; (b) While creating an environment and encouraging innovation is important to encourage alternative livelihood options, most of the households who received small loans only invested in a limited range of opportunities (broom-making, fish sauce production, vegetable cultivation), which lead to market saturation, a factor that is exacerbated by the distance between Quang Ngai and major economic hubs; and (c) It is critical to accompany livelihood diversification activities with technical skills to ensure adaptive capacity building, as not all livelihood initiatives were successful due to lack of labor, knowledge, land, and market linkages required to sustain new livelihoods.

Some of the income-generation activities that participants pursued, such as growing bamboo shoots near the river bank, were not successful because the bamboo shoots were inundated before they were established. This shows that access to assets alone is not sufficient to build adaptive capacity. This project assumed that people had the labor, knowledge, land and market linkages required to benefit from sales of bamboo and household goods. Growing bamboo shoots requires a level of technical knowledge and is a long-term investment; this proved to be a challenge for some communities that did not have the time to focus on long-term investments as they needed income quickly.

FAQs

What is the difference between disaster risk reduction and climate change adaptation?

Disaster risk reduction and climate change adaptation have similar aims and mutual benefits, and are thus closely linked. Both focus on reducing people's vulnerability to hazards by improving their ability to anticipate, cope with and recover from the impact; and, because climate change increases the frequency and intensity of climate-related hazards, the use of a disaster risk reduction approach is crucial in supporting communities to adapt to climate change.

Not all disaster hazards are climate-related. Climate-related (or hydro-meteorological) hazards include floods, droughts and storms, although disaster risk reduction applies equally to geological hazards (e.g. earthquakes, tsunamis, and volcanoes), technological hazards (e.g. industrial, chemical spills) and conflict. And equally, climate change impacts are not all hazards. They include the longer-term effects that will affect communities over time such as rising temperature, changing seasonal patterns, unpredictable rainfall patterns and rising sea-level, and the flow-on effects to food and nutrition security, health and poverty in general.

What is the difference between climate and weather?

The difference is the timescale. Weather refers to conditions like rain, temperature and wind over hours to days. Climate refers to those average weather conditions measured over a much longer period (30+ years).

How do we deal with uncertainty in climate forecasts?

Although climate forecasts are uncertain, the broad conclusions of climate change science are based on many lines of evidence which together give a high degree of confidence that the Earth is warming due to increases in greenhouse gas in the atmosphere caused by human activities. Partly because of scientific uncertainty, but also because many aspects of human life are involved, decisions about action on climate change will need to involve extensive consideration of issues beyond science, including social, economic and environmental.

Is adapting to climate change the only option?

No. In order to address climate change, the world also has to address its underlying causes—greenhouse gas pollution. If the current trajectory of emissions continues then the average global temperature could rise by two to three degrees Celsius in the next 50 years; by the end of the century it could exceed five or six degrees (Stern Review on the Economics of Climate Change, 2006). This could lead to a variety of severe impacts: from the melting of permafrost and the loss of tropical rainforests (both stores of carbon); the loss of almost all tropical glaciers; and the melting of the polar ice caps. Stopping accelerated warming once a two- or three-degree temperature threshold is reached would become extremely difficult.

Thus the critical issue facing humanity is how to drastically reduce emissions to keep global warming below dangerous levels. This requires a great effort by all countries.

However, while everyone can help to reduce emissions, many of the people who are most affected by climate change produce only a small percentage of the world's total emissions, making their adaptation to potential effects a priority.

Is disaster risk reduction realistic in humanitarian responses?

Even in situations of urgent need, humanitarian aid can be provided in ways that build on people's own capacities as individuals, households and communities and that strengthen the capacities of local institutions. For example, cash distributions enable people to balance meeting emergency needs with conserving livelihoods assets, thereby avoiding actions that would make them more vulnerable. When international organizations work with local organizations to distribute emergency relief, such as temporary or transitional shelter materials, not only does the distribution benefit from local knowledge, but the local organizations gain experience in disaster response that may help them to improve disaster preparedness[G] measures in their communities. Humanitarian aid is effectively provided in such ways in many different disaster situations and is a realistic expectation. See *5.2 Early recovery from a humanitarian crisis* section, for further guidance.

In slow-onset disasters there are even greater opportunities to reduce both present and future disaster risk. Development and humanitarian organizations can provide assistance that enables people to reduce their risk of falling sick by, for example, rehabilitating water sources in drought-affected areas, and providing information and chlorine for making water safe for drinking in flood situations. They can also provide technical support to strengthen early warning systems[G], improve evacuation procedures, and build the capacity of local authorities to assess and reduce risks. See *5.4 Slow-onset disasters* section, for further guidance.

Several of the Core Standards of Sphere Minimum Standards in Humanitarian Response are relevant for disaster risk reduction. Further guidance on relevant and realistic actions, indicators and guidance notes can be found in *The Sphere Handbook* (See *Tools and resources* p.135).

Tools and resources

For information and links, see *Tools and resources* p.133.

2

KEY GROUPS
FOR DISASTER RISK REDUCTION
AND CLIMATE CHANGE ADAPTATION

Chapter 2 is designed to help development and humanitarian practitioners understand how specific population groups—children, men, women, and certain high-risk groups—tend to experience disaster and climate change risk, and how they can contribute to building resilience^G. It is intended to generate awareness of differential vulnerability^G by presenting selected examples. Practitioners are encouraged to use the *Checklist* at the end of this chapter to analyze issues relating to other potentially high-risk groups in specific contexts.

Chapter 2 includes:

- *Explanations* of the nature and causes of risk experienced by each group.
- *Examples* of the types of programs and advocacy actions that benefit each group.
- *Answers* to frequently asked questions.
- A *checklist* for ensuring the participation of, and action by, key groups within the population at risk.

2.1 Children

Wherever disaster risk^G is high for the population in general, it is likely to be higher for children.[14]

In rapid-onset events, such as earthquakes and landslides, children in schools whose construction is not hazard-resilient are particularly vulnerable. Following all types of disaster^G events, including those that are low-profile and low-impact, such as regular flooding and drought, children's future wellbeing is also likely to be compromised by a reduction in household income, disruption to education, and loss or sickness of family members on whom they depend.[15] In households experiencing severe economic hardship, adolescent girls may be forced into early marriage or prostitution, and adolescent boys may be drawn into delinquency.

The growing intensity and frequency of climate-related hazards[G], as well as longer-term climate change[G], and their potential harm to food and nutrition security, health and basic services, will also take a disproportionately heavy toll on children as malnutrition and ill health during childhood impede future learning and physical development.[16]

Children have the right to be protected, and to participate in decisions that affect their lives.[17] They also have the capacity[G] to be energetic and influential proponents of disaster risk reduction[G] and climate change adaptation[G] in their families, schools and communities and should be encouraged to participate in resilience-building interventions.

Box 2.1: Examples of disaster risk reduction and climate change adaptation programming with a child-centered approach

- Training and resources for institutions responsible for disaster risk reduction and climate change adaptation to involve children and young people in program design and implementation, impact monitoring, and policy-making.
- School-feeding programs during and after cyclical hazards, to prevent malnutrition and provide incentives for families to keep children in school.
- Social protection/cash transfer measures for families to reduce existing vulnerabilities.
- Engagement of youth clubs and children's groups in participatory risk assessments.
- Facilitation of children's involvement in the design and development of national policies for disaster management, child welfare and climate change adaptation.
- Structural strengthening of schools in relation to known hazards and the projected local effects of climate change.
- Contingency plans for education and service provision in relation to known hazards and the projected local effects of climate change.
- Child-focused theatre, comic books and other visual media to explain the causes and effects of disaster and climate change risk.
- Murals depicting risk reduction and adaptation practices, such as evacuation procedures, water conservation and treatment, hygiene, protection of livestock, etc.
- Age-appropriate participation of children and young people in local projects to build resilience, such as maintaining coastal mangroves, cleaning water pans in drought-prone areas, planting saplings on exposed hillsides, etc.
- The use of participatory video as a way to engage children in disaster risk reduction and climate change adaptation activities.

FAQs

Who is considered a child?

The Convention on the Rights of the Child states that a child is an individual under the age of 18 years. This definition can differ depending on cultural and social contexts. A thorough analysis of how at-risk and affected populations define children should be undertaken, to ensure that all children and young people can exercise their right to protection[G], and participate in analysis and decision-making processes on disaster risk reduction and climate change adaptation issues.

What are the benefits of involving children in actions to reduce disaster and climate change risk?

Children usually make up more than half the population in vulnerable communities, urban neighborhoods and countries. Involving them in its design and implementation increases the likelihood of a resilience-building program or policy being responsive to their needs. As children interact with other children and adults, if they are well-informed and supported, they can be effective channels of information, role models and agents of change. Also, by developing children's understanding of risk and ways to manage it, interventions are more likely to have a sustainable impact in the medium- to long-term.

What are some of the obstacles to involving children in actions to reduce disaster and climate change risk, and how can they be overcome?

In some cultures children are not encouraged or empowered to share their views, out of respect for elders. Awareness of the rationale for, and the benefits of, involving children in disaster risk reduction and climate change adaptation activities, as well as adults should be raised among the population in general.

In other cases, parents may be anxious that their children could be put in danger if they engage in such activities, either directly or because groups with vested interests in maintaining the status quo may target them if they speak up. It is critical to analyze the potential impacts of children's involvement before instigating any action, and to ensure that child protection is paramount.

Other more practical considerations include designing activities to fit in with, or around, children's school schedules, work and domestic duties.

What creates an enabling environment that facilitates children's participation in disaster risk reduction and climate change adaptation programming?

Factors include: the level of awareness of risk in the community or neighborhood; the disposition of teachers, religious leaders and other people in authority to engage in discussion on risk factors and risk reduction; the organization of the community or neighborhood; the existence and knowledge of laws on child protection and welfare; government policies and budgets for inclusive participation from national to local levels; attitudes towards children (particularly girls) voicing their opinions and taking part in collective activities. For further guidance on creating an enabling environment, consult *Chapter 6: Creating an enabling environment for disaster risk reduction and climate change adaptation.*

CASE STUDY: SUMMER CAMP EXERCISE HELPS CHILDREN FEEL MORE SAFE AND SECURE[18]

Philippines, Save the Children

Jessica is a Grade 4 pupil at Manila Elementary School in a high-risk municipality in Albay, near the Mayon Volcano on the Philippines' Luzon Island. She is one of the many children who witnessed the devastation of Typhoon Durian in November, 2006, that caused massive deaths due to mudslides from loosened slopes of the nearby volcano. Jessica and 616 other pupils from 22 high-risk public elementary schools attended the Children's Summer Camp sponsored by the Bicol Assistance Project being implemented by Save the Children with funding support from USAID to learn how to prepare for and respond to disasters thus **increasing their understanding of the hazard and climate change context**.

Jessica is interested in the project because she lives only eight kilometers from the volcano, the most active in the Bicol Region. She is also well aware that her family and community constantly face the risks associated with typhoons, landslides, flash floods, earthquakes, fire, and volcanic hazards.

At the camp, she participates in a drill scenario of a 7.5 magnitude earthquake that also triggers a fire that results in mass "casualties" on the campus. After hearing the blast that signals the simulated earthquake, she and the rest of the campers immediately duck, cover their heads with their hands, and seek safety under sturdy tables and chairs as they have been taught. As one of the key leaders of the Bulilit Emergency Response Team (BERT) in her school during the camp, Jessica leads the way out of the classroom to the safe holding area after hearing the evacuation warning bells and rapid whistles.

Once in the safe area, she listens carefully to the principal-turned-incident-commander's instructions to the school's Emergency Response Team Security Committees and its Disaster Risk Reduction Management Group to perform an immediate head count and to form a human cordon around panicking pupils. The principal asks an adult search and rescue team to do a sweep of classrooms and transfer victims to the safe area. Jessica realizes it is critical that children are not involved in the search and rescue, and that the adults will be trained in these tasks in keeping with the Convention on the Rights of the Child. Like other responders, Jessica performs basic first aid on her classmate. After the victim has received first aid, Jessica asks other students to help her move the victims from the first aid area to the ambulance for transport to the nearest hospital.

Besides a team of trained teachers, the exercise was made possible by project partners from the Philippine National Red Cross, Municipal Emergency Response and Interventions Teams, Municipal Disaster Coordinating Council, Bureau of Fire Protection, and the Albay Mabuhay Task Force.

Jessica said the summer camp experience had shown her that she could help save lives, and also made other children feel more safe and secure.

Tools and resources

For information and links, see *Tools and resources* p.136.

2.2 Women and men

Disaster and climate change risks are not gender-neutral. The nature and extent of their exposure[G] and vulnerability is different for women, men, girls and boys because of their different roles, responsibilities, access to resources, domestic and traditional law, and legal and cultural issues. For example:

- Women may be less able to evacuate to a safe place following a hazard because they are pregnant or caring for children and less-mobile dependents. Their exposure, and that of their dependents, may be much greater than that of others who are able to leave high-risk areas.

- Women's lack of formal land ownership may prevent them from accessing credit to introduce climate-adaptive measures in their livelihoods[G], invest in appropriate building materials or ability to move to a safer location.

- A decline in the productivity of traditional rural livelihoods may put men under pressure to migrate in search of work, or to undertake higher-risk livelihood activities in order to continue to provide for their families.

- Boys/men may not know how to feed and care for young children if required to take on these roles if women in the household are killed or injured as a result of a disaster event.

The root causes of women's vulnerability often lie in unequal power relations within societies, which pervades all aspects of their lives and deny their basic rights, from access to education to participation in community governance[G]. Their vulnerability may also be conditioned by cultural roles that restrict them from developing knowledge and skills that would enable them to save lives and prevent disaster losses, such as learning to swim, or participating in public meetings. This, in turn, affects other vulnerable members of their households.

In most societies, men's vulnerability is also closely associated with cultural expectations. Many men are conditioned to feel that it is their duty to meet their family's basic needs and, when they are unable to do so, they may resort to dangerous work, or migration to seek employment elsewhere, or turn to alcohol or substance abuse.

Women's and men's capacities for building disaster and climate resilience are shaped by their social, cultural, economic, and natural resource management[G] roles. For example:

- Women often have a major influence on the behavior of children and other members of their households, as well as of the wider community, and can therefore play a key role in reducing risk by ensuring safe food storage, adopting climate-appropriate practices for water consumption and hygiene, and preparing for adverse conditions.

- In many cultures, men spend more time outside the home and may receive public early warning messages before women and children. They can reduce risk for their families by passing on this information as quickly as possible.

- Both mothers and fathers pass on traditional livelihoods knowledge and skills to their sons and daughters, including how to manage risk through diverse income-generating activities, and how to adapt to different weather patterns or fluctuations in market conditions.

- Women and men may have specific knowledge about the management of natural resources critical for their livelihoods, and may therefore have unique skills in adapting these in the face of climate change.

Crises and stresses[G] also offer opportunities for women and men to challenge socially conditioned gender[G] roles and power structures, such as community leadership roles in negotiations with local government on priorities for adaptation, or as recipients of financial assistance for disaster-recovery. In such situations, building disaster and climate resilience can offer win-win outcomes in terms of risk management and gender equity.

Box 2.2: Examples of gender-sensitive disaster risk reduction and climate change adaptation programming

- Ensuring that women and men participate in planning processes, training and drills for early warning and evacuations.
- Providing safety-net cash transfers for household food security and basic needs directly to women.
- Providing fodder and veterinary attention for animals traditionally kept by women and men.
- Facilitating consultation of women and men in participatory risk analyses, and generating inputs from both with respect to their resilience-building priorities.
- Supporting research on gendered impacts of disaster and climate change risk and successful practices in gender-sensitive programming.
- Facilitating access to appropriate credit facilities and training to women and men for adapting their livelihoods to changing conditions.
- Involving women and men in the development of land-use policies, to generate awareness of high-risk areas and opportunities for relocation.
- Providing legal support to women and men to get birth certificates, ID cards and registry titles, to enable them to claim their rights and participate in political processes to their benefit.

FAQs

Who is more at risk; women or men? Is this different for disasters and climate change?

The nature and extent of disaster and climate change risk for women and men is different in every location and set of circumstances. In terms of mortality following hazards, in Hurricane Mitch (1998), more men than women died because men were more involved in rescue efforts, while in the Indian Ocean Tsunami (2004) more women than men died because they were less likely to know how to swim and their long clothing hampered their movement.[19] But being at risk includes other types of potential losses, such as losing livelihood assets, housing, health and wellbeing. Following the Peru earthquake of 2007, the unemployment rate rose more sharply for women than for men as key production and service industries which had employed them were affected, whereas in rural Australia repeated flooding and drought events are reported to be impacting more heavily on men's mental health and suicide rates than on those of women.[20] A study of the 2007 floods in Nepal found that women in particular were affected by anxiety, sleeplessness and feelings of helplessness as a result of their displacement and a loss of social networks they depended on.[21]

To ensure that programs are gender-sensitive, risk assessments should involve men and women, and relevant data should be disaggregated by sex as well as other variables (age, livelihood type, location etc.) to the greatest extent possible. Gender considerations and gender-differentiated impacts of the program should continue to be monitored and addressed at all stages of the program cycle. Use the *Checklist* of this section for further guidance.

In cultures where women do not feel empowered to put forward their views, particularly in public, how can they be sufficiently involved in disaster risk reduction and climate change adaptation actions?

If one does not already exist, a gender analysis of the social, economic, political, and natural resource management roles of women, men, boys and girls should be carried out before starting other activities. This will provide baseline information for programming, and can also be used to generate discussion on the results. For this, and throughout the program, focus group meetings should be held with separate gender groups, women and men should be interviewed independently, surveys should be conducted in ways that provide disaggregated data, and facilitation methods in mixed gender meetings should enable men and women to make contributions. Not all disaster risk reduction and climate change adaptation action involves speaking in public forums. Risk reduction measures are taken at all levels, from the household up to national policy making, and in all areas of daily life, from water collection to harvesting crops and practicing emergency drills in factories and schools. There are multiple opportunities for participation of women and men, both within and outside of their cultural or traditional roles.

Tools and resources

For information and links, see *Tools and resources* p.137.

2.3   High-risk groups

Certain physical, social and cultural factors are likely to make certain groups of people more exposed and vulnerable to hazards and the effects of climate change.

People with disabilities

Disabilities are mental and physical impairments that limit a person's cognitive ability, mobility and activity. Women, men and children with disabilities are often excluded from aspects of a community's daily life because of a lack of awareness or assumptions made by other members of that community. They may not be asked to participate in discussions about the risks^G that face the community, and therefore may not be able to help identify risk reduction and adaptation measures that could be carried out by, and be effective for, people living with disabilities.

People with limited cognitive ability are particularly vulnerable to rapid-onset hazards. For example, they may have a limited understanding of what an early warning signal for a tsunami means, and may not react in time to be safely evacuated. People with limited mobility, for example, are likely to be very vulnerable in contexts of increasing water scarcity, as they may not be able to access more distant water points.

All people living with disabilities have capacities for activities that are of benefit to them and others. In many cultures, female family members with physical disabilities are a constant presence in the home and are responsible for some aspects of childcare. In such roles, they have capacity to educate children on risk and risk-reducing practices. Men and women with limited mobility are also able to act as a focal point for information collection and provision to the wider community, such as on rainfall monitoring or early warning messaging.

Box 2.3: Examples of disaster risk reduction and climate change adaptation programming that is inclusive of people living with disabilities

- Setting up neighbor-support networks to assist people with mental and physical disabilities in the event of evacuation, relief distribution and other disaster management activities.
- Situating wells and aid distribution points in locations that are accessible to people with restricted mobility.
- Providing fuel-efficient stoves to households with people with restricted mobility.
- Providing livelihood-diversification grants and training to people with disabilities whose traditional livelihood activities are at risk from hazards and/or the effects of climate change.

People living with chronic diseases

Chronic diseases such as HIV and AIDS, tuberculosis and malaria, have a significant effect on how households and communities are affected by disaster risk. For example, affected households (including elderly and child-headed households) are likely to be deficient in the manual labor and investment required for preparing for a flood, or recovering from a drought, due to sickness among adult members, income-poverty and the strain of additional expenses for healthcare or funerals. For the same reasons, children of affected households are likely to have poor nutritional and health status and therefore be more vulnerable to diseases that become more prevalent in a changing climate.

When a disaster disrupts or causes damage to services, people living with HIV and AIDS may no longer have access to vital treatment, and if the disruption is prolonged, it can accelerate the progression of the virus. People with other chronic diseases may also struggle to get the medication on which they depend.

Chronic diseases also affect households' and communities' capacity to adapt to climate change. People are often income-insecure and therefore resist innovating or diversifying their livelihoods because they perceive the risk of failure to be greater than the risks they face on a day-to-day basis. Children in affected households are likely to have lower literacy rates because they have taken on productive or care-giving roles instead of attending school. Consequently, they are likely to have low incomes and have reduced life chances.

Box 2.4: Examples of disaster risk reduction and climate change adaptation programming inclusive of people living with chronic diseases

- Facilitating participation of people and households affected by other chronic diseases in risk assessments, training on disaster and climate reduction, and involvement in collaborative activities to reduce risk. See *Checklist* in section 2.4 for ways to facilitate the participation of high-risk groups.
- Intervening early with targeted cash transfers and/or food aid to affected households to prevent food insecurity during hazards such as droughts and other critical periods.
- Tailoring hygiene-promotion messaging and inputs to reduce the risk of secondary infections during hazards such as floods and displacement to temporary shelters.
- Ensuring the physical protection (retrofitting) of health facilities and coordination with health personnel to sustain continuity of services during hazards.
- Developing contingency plans with health facilities to ensure uninterrupted access to medicines during hazards and climate stresses.

Older people

In general, older age can result in decreased mobility and muscle strength. These physical limitations may prevent older people from preparing for hazards by, for example, raising floor levels to cope with floods, or boarding up windows to reduce the likelihood and extent of hurricane damage. Physical limitations may also prevent older people from adopting risk reduction and adaptation measures that require manual labor, such as planting trees to reduce soil erosion around crop lands, and, in the event of an emergency, it may also impede their escape.

Older men and women with poor health also have greater susceptibility to diseases, some of which—such as malaria and cholera—are common in the aftermath of disasters, and predicted to become more widespread as a result of climate change. Older people are also more likely to experience health complications (and even death) during temperature extremes.

Many older people and, in particular, older women, are physically, socially and emotionally reliant on family and community support structures. While such networks are normally considered to be assets, they can be significantly weakened by displacement, migration, asset loss/erosion and other impacts of disasters and climate change if efforts are not made to reinforce them.

Nevertheless, older people's knowledge of the community history, layout and demographics can be an asset to any project and community/neighborhood, and they may be well-placed to identify other vulnerable people. Some older men and women may have a greater knowledge of traditional coping measures and risk-reducing practices, such as community grain banks, water-harvesting or mixed cropping, some of which may be adapted and applied. Older women often play a key role in childcare, allowing productive generations to invest time and energy in new risk reduction or adaptive strategies.

Box 2.5: Examples of disaster risk reduction and climate change adaptation programming inclusive of older people

- Establishing community networks that assist older people living alone to protect their houses and assets from impending hazards such as storms and floods.
- Targeting health and hygiene support to older people (advice and material inputs such as bed nets, chlorine, etc.) to reduce risks of falling sick due to unsanitary conditions caused by flooding, displacement, and other hazards.
- Preparing contingency plans with health service providers to ensure continuity of operations during and after hazards.
- Facilitating participation of older people in community risk assessment, knowledge-sharing and decision-making processes.
- Involving older people in components of community early warning systems, such as operating community radio stations, transmitting alert/evacuation messages, recording river levels, etc.

Indigenous peoples

The majority of the world's 300 million indigenous peoples are poor and marginalized.[22] Many live in isolated areas outside the mainstream of international markets, national economies and development support. Their lands, for which formal tenure is often a contested issue, tend to lack basic infrastructure such as roads, schools and health posts.[23]

The economic poverty of many indigenous peoples is compounded by 'voice poverty'—marginalization from national or regional decision-making processes that have a direct impact on their lives. Linguistic and cultural differences can further isolate them from the majority.

The weak economic and political status of many indigenous peoples makes them vulnerable to the impacts of hazards. Also, the ecosystems on which many depend for their livelihoods and basic needs—high altitudes, humid tropics, deserts and arid areas, polar regions and small islands—are among those most exposed to the effects of climate change.

However, through intergenerational transmission of knowledge, indigenous peoples have detected, and adapted to, climate variability[G] and local-level climate change over thousands of years. Their knowledge of traditional coping strategies offer them important foundations for resilience and adaptive capacity[G] that could be enhanced in an enabling environment that respects and promotes their rights.

Box 2.6: Examples of disaster risk reduction and climate change adaptation programming to strengthen the resilience of indigenous peoples

- Supporting legal recognition of indigenous peoples' collective and intergenerational rights to their territories and natural resources, as the basis for livelihood security, cultural identity and political leverage.

- Promoting access to financial resources for development of basic services in indigenous territories.

- Developing educational and informative materials in appropriate media on the causes of disaster and climate change risk, and measures to reduce it.

- Encouraging forums within and between indigenous communities to identify and share traditional mechanisms for coping with climate variability and natural hazards, and to analyse their potential effectiveness in future climate change scenarios.

- Promoting access to technology and scientific knowledge generated by non-indigenous peoples.

- Integrating participation into regional early warning mechanisms through linguistically and culturally appropriate mechanisms.

CASE STUDY: KEYHOLE GARDEN LEARNING INITIATIVE FOR DISASTER RISK REDUCTION[24]

Lesotho, Catholic Relief Services

Even where enough food is grown to cater for people's caloric needs, dietary diversity is crucial to maintaining good health and resilience to external shocks[G] such as illness or periodic poor harvests. In many parts of the world, traditional diets are low in diversity and nutrient content, relying heavily on starches such as maize or cassava, one or two types of leafy vegetables and occasionally some protein, usually plant-derived. In addition, vegetables are often highly seasonal, such that micronutrient intake may not be reliable throughout the year.

Eighty percent of the world's cropland is rain-fed and, in times of drought, in Southern Africa alone, tens of millions of people may require food aid. As climate change contributes to growing uncertainty about rainfall and other weather patterns, many parts of the world may begin to experience more drought, flooding, changes in crop yields, and more or different pests. Strategies are needed not only to provide methods of growing sufficient staple crops in dry areas, but also to maximize the benefits to vulnerable people of what water is available.

Climate change-induced effects in Lesotho are expected to have a far-reaching regional impact on regional fresh water resources as the country is a major source of fresh water, and drainage areas extend into the Atlantic basin through South Africa, Namibia and Botswana. Climate-related stresses have been prevalent in Lesotho for a long time. The people of Lesotho have evolved within this climatic context and have developed a range of coping mechanisms which have served them well but what has changed in recent times is the apparent increasing frequency, magnitude and duration of climatic shocks, leaving little or no time to recover from the last event.

From 2005 to 2008, the USAID/Food for Peace-funded Consortium for Southern Africa Food Emergency (C-SAFE) program in Lesotho promoted homestead gardens, including keyhole gardens, among populations vulnerable to food insecurity as a way to improve household resilience to external shocks such as drought. Keyhole gardens use local materials and are built in a circle about two meters in diameter and one meter high with a "keyhole" entry into the center so the gardener can stand to work on the entire plot with little effort. A composting basket is placed in the center of the "keyhole" where gray water from washing dishes and clothes or bathing is used to irrigate through the basket, in order to conserve water and reduce the labor burden of collecting extra water for irrigation. Thatching grass, reeds, or other materials used to construct the basket help filter chemicals in soaps and detergents from the gray water. The garden is built using layers of organic material that serve the dual purpose of adding nutrients to the soil and retaining moisture, making the keyhole garden extremely productive even in the cold, dry winter months. Once built, the garden requires only limited maintenance and few additional inputs (such as fertilizer). In addition, the layer-based design helps the garden retain moisture, so it requires less water.

There are multiple benefits of keyhole gardening in building the resilience of poor households: Labor-saving technology; moisture retention in arid or semi-arid climates; soil-nutrient enrichment; improved nutrition; year-round vegetable production; reduced dependence on external input; and increased income from sales of surplus production.

Communities participate in the construction of the gardens, gathering the materials and building the structures. In Lesotho, community members build gardens for those most in need and continue construction as a collective group for vulnerable families, thereby benefiting the entire community. By fully involving the community in all aspects of the construction—identifying the location, gathering the materials and building the garden—the process **strengthens the participation of, and action by, the population at risk**. Community members learn to build and maintain the gardens so they can continue to construct additional gardens as they wish.

Keyhole gardens can play an important role in disaster risk reduction as they build the resilience of smallholder farmers to water scarcity, while encouraging dietary diversity and providing opportunities for generating cash income. The methodology has been successfully tested and widely adopted in Lesotho but has not yet become widely known or adopted elsewhere, despite its enormous potential to boost household resilience across Africa and beyond.

Given the success of keyhole gardens in decreasing the vulnerability of households to external shocks such as drought, while increasing food security for people made vulnerable by labor constraints—such as the elderly, the young, people living with HIV or AIDS, and the disabled—in 2012, CRS launched a project to expand learning and test the adaptation of the methodology to other parts of the world. At the project launch event, representatives from NGOs, the UN, local government bodies, academics and scientists from 17 countries came together to learn about the experiences with the methodology in Lesotho, engage in the construction of keyhole gardens, and to generate ideas on how the practice could be adapted in their own country context. Ideas included the use of locally available materials, such as bamboo, for the exterior walls, rather than the rock used in Lesotho and the promotion of the design in crowded areas such as urban neighborhoods and in IDP or refugee camps.

The outcome of this learning initiative, a handbook for practitioners and a short training film, were published in September 2012. Both materials incorporate the recommended local adaptations and best practices.

The project is demonstrating that: 1) There are ways to adapt methodology so that similar homestead gardens reduce disaster risk reduction and promote climate change adaptation; 2) There is great interest in promoting the methodology given the experiences in Lesotho, though adaptation is not always easy; 3) It is important to take a participatory approach to beneficiary selection, community engagement and to include sustainability in the selection criteria for targets and partners; and 4) Keyhole gardens should be promoted within integrated development programs for food security and disaster risk reduction initiatives.

CRS Lesotho has expanded the construction of keyhole gardens to address food and nutritional needs of other vulnerable groups, including orphans and vulnerable children and people living with HIV.

FAQs

Are there other high-risk groups? If so, how should their particular needs and rights be taken into account?

Every context is different; hence the economic, social, physical, cultural and political factors that put different groups at higher risk than others are different. Some other high-risk groups are religious minorities, ethnic minorities, refugees, displaced people, illegal immigrants, low-caste people and outcasts, and people with lifestyles involving non-conventional sexuality.

Use existing knowledge of the population to identify potentially high-risk groups, and follow the steps in the *Checklist* provided below to ensure they are fully considered, consulted on decisions and involved in appropriate activities throughout the program.

Tools and resources

For information and links, see *Tools and resources* p.138.

2.4 Checklist for participation of, and action by, key groups

The rights, needs and contribution of all people at risk, especially those at high risk, should be included into all stages of disaster risk reduction and climate change adaptation programs and advocacy. This checklist is intended to assist practitioners in this process, and is to be used with the guidance for applying the principles in all sectors and contexts.

Checklist for participation and agency of key groups

- Obtain or build a **demographic profile** of the target population and related stakeholders, ensuring that all data is disaggregated by sex, age, and other relevant groups as presented in this chapter.

- Ensure that staff understand and act in accordance with a rights-based approach[G], and that they are aware of the relevant international and national legal frameworks for the target population. Build staff capacity to promote this approach with partners, governments and other actors.

- Use a **participatory methodology** for all stages in the program cycle, from risk assessment to evaluations, and ensure that the participation of all high-risk groups identified in the demographic profile is facilitated. This may involve arranging activities at times convenient to them, providing logistical or financial support so that they can attend meetings, providing an interpreter, etc.

- Make the involvement of key groups central to the **design and implementation** of programs and advocacy, and prioritize strategies and actions that will benefit high-risk groups.

- Continue to **disaggregate data** for analysis and decision-making purposes throughout the program and advocacy cycles, using the same groups identified at the outset and any others.

3

PROGRAM CYCLE MANAGEMENT
FOR DISASTER RISK REDUCTION
AND CLIMATE CHANGE ADAPTATION

Chapter 3 is designed to help development and humanitarian practitioners design, implement, monitor and evaluate programs that build disaster and climate resilience[G]. It is equally applicable for programs whose principal focus is disaster risk reduction[G] and climate change adaptation[G], and for multi-sectoral or sector-specific interventions that require integration of disaster risk reduction and climate change adaptation. This chapter is adapted from: CARE (2010) *Community-Based Adaptation Toolkit*. This chapter includes:

- An *overview* of program cycle management.
- *Guidance* for practitioners at each stage of the program cycle, including key steps, activities and outputs related to monitoring, evaluation and learning[G] (MEL), and knowledge management.
- *Examples* of good practice.
- *Guidance for applying the 10 principles* for integrated disaster risk reduction and climate change adaptation in program cycle management.

3.1 Overview of program cycle management

Program cycle management (PCM) is the term used to describe the management of activities and decision-making procedures used during the life cycle of a program. It emphasizes the cyclical, recurring nature of programming, as well as the interdependency of actions within an intervention throughout the different phases.

This guide uses a simplified program cycle model with three main phases—analysis, design and implementation—each with corresponding activities and outputs. Central and continuous throughout the program cycle is knowledge generation and management that incorporates monitoring and evaluation and supports the transition between each of the stages. While there are other types of PCM in existence, and many organizations have their own models, the key components—such as separate phases to facilitate planning, and the cyclical nature of the process—are likely to remain the same. The process outlined in the guide includes:

- Establishing program-specific baselines, as well as baseline information relevant to the external environment;
- Setting and monitoring indicators of change;
- Reviewing and evaluating progress and achievements against planned results, and using these to continually improve the program, and
- Capturing and sharing the knowledge generated to support learning.

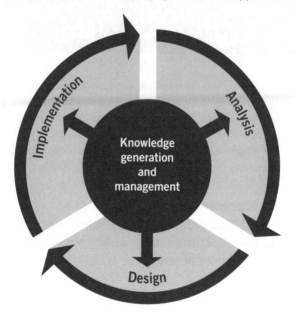

Figure 3.1: Stages of the program cycle

Central to PCM is the active participation of at-risk populations because programs will only be effective if they are based on the needs of those at risk from disasters[G] and climate change[G]. PCM should therefore aim to:

- Seek full inclusion of at-risk populations in all levels of planning, as well as implementation, monitoring and evaluation processes (by providing, for example, information in local languages);
- Understand and address at-risk populations' unique needs through targeted interventions;
- Ensure that disaster risk reduction and climate change adaptation activities do not inadvertently worsen their vulnerability[G];
- Redress power imbalances and other structural causes of differential exposure[G] and vulnerability within and between households.[25]

3.2 Analysis

The *purpose* of the analysis stage is to: 1) gather relevant information so that stakeholders[G] gain a better understanding of the nature and extent of disaster and climate change risk in the context of a new or ongoing program (problem identification); and 2) to ensure that programming continues to be relevant to the needs of targeted at-risk populations.

Specifically, this stage should generate knowledge from a variety of sources of:

- Hazards[G] and climate conditions that have typically occurred in the target area.

- Observed and projected changes in hazards and climate conditions.

- The impact of current and future hazards and climate change (including the levels of certainty) on at-risk populations living in the target area, and on the resources upon which they depend.

- The effectiveness of current strategies employed by at-risk populations to manage disaster and climate change risk, and their sustainability in the context of future climate scenarios.

- Social groups and livelihoods[G] that are particularly vulnerable to current and future hazards and climate conditions.

- Government policies and programs that facilitate or impede disaster risk reduction and climate change adaptation.

- Priority issues identified by the target population for disaster risk reduction and climate change adaptation programming.

- Potential partners, allies and opponents for disaster risk reduction and climate change adaptation programming.

- The capacity[G] development needs of staff and partners who may be responsible for designing, implementing and monitoring any potential program.

- Other initiatives that may complement or coincide with potential programs.

The *timeframe* of the analysis stage may be adapted according to the circumstances of each program. For example, the initial stages of a disaster response and recovery program requires rapid, 'good enough' analysis that can be improved during program implementation, whereas a long-term development program typically allows a longer analysis and planning stage. However, whatever the program duration, the possible longer-term impacts of climate change should be taken into account to ensure that any intervention is sustainable over the longer term, even after the program has ended.

The *scope* of the analysis process should be adapted to the scope of potential programming. For example, if the purpose of the analysis is to create a local development plan, it should be multi-sectoral, whereas if the analysis aims to inform a new stage of a food security program, it may focus mainly on issues that affect livelihoods and nutrition.

Key steps in the analysis stage

There are five key steps in the analysis stage:

1. *Define the analysis purpose and process*:

   - Discuss and agree among the main stakeholders (including at-risk populations and potential partners) the purpose of analyzing disaster and climate change risk in broad terms, and how the results of the analysis will be used. This could include the development of new stand-alone disaster risk reduction and/or climate change adaptation programs, and the redesign of existing programs to include disaster risk reduction and/or climate change adaptation components to improve their effectiveness.

   - Decide how the analysis will be undertaken: by whom; over what period; which sources of information will be used; and how stakeholders will be involved.

   - Ensure that the process includes data collection from primary (community members, meteorological services) and secondary (official statistics, research reports) sources.

   - Identify a participatory risk analysis tool or a variety of participatory research techniques for local-level analysis, and customize it/them as necessary, to ensure the needs of at-risk populations are central to the analysis.

   - Ensure that all facilitators of the process are familiar with the chosen methodology.

2. *Analyze the hazard and climate context*:

   - Collect data from primary and secondary sources on:
     - Historical climate conditions and projected climate change scenarios in the target area (or at the lowest available scale).
     - Climate and non-climate related hazard occurrence in the target population and surrounding area.

   - Consult different socio-economic and livelihoods groups within the target population about:
     - Observations of changing climate conditions in their lifetime.
     - Hazards affecting their community and the surrounding area in their lifetime.

- Analyze the effects of the above on the assets, resources and facilities on which community members' wellbeing and livelihoods depend.

- Analyze how current and future hazard and climate scenarios may affect any existing programs in the area.

- Analyze how information provided by climate information providers is understood and applied by the target population (and how it could be improved) and include this in baseline information.

Box 3.1: Examples of primary and secondary sources of climate information

- Local weather stations
- Community knowledge and local forecasting
- National meteorological services
- Government climate change departments
- Regional climate centres
- International climate institutions

---

3. *Analyze capacities for resilience, and vulnerability within the target population to understand:*

- How different groups and sectors of the population currently deal with hazards and climate variability^G, and how effective and sustainable their methods are.

- The potential impact of any current programs on the above.

- The groups and sectors of the population which are, and are likely to be, most vulnerable to hazards and effects of climate change.

- The reasons for their vulnerability, from the conditions in which they live and work, to underlying factors such as access to resources, political influence and social structures.

- How vulnerabilities, capacities and coping mechanisms have changed over time.

4. *Analyze the programming environment by conducting a power analysis:*

- Identify the opportunities and obstacles for disaster risk reduction and climate change adaptation created by governmental and non-governmental programs being implemented in, or being planned for, the target area.

- Identify any relevant governmental policies and/or policy gaps that may affect vulnerability and resilience^G among the target population.

- Identify any private sector activities that present opportunities and obstacles for disaster risk reduction and climate change adaptation.

- Analyze the interest of governmental, non-governmental and private sector organizations in disaster risk reduction and climate change adaptation, and their capacity for action (plans, structures, activities).

5. *Validate and document the analysis, and establish a contextual baseline*:

- Discuss, amend (if necessary), and engage stakeholders to validate the results of the analysis.
- Document the process (data sources and analysis methods) and results, including any gaps, and share with key stakeholders, especially the target population.
- Select key data to form a contextual baseline against which to measure trends in hazard occurrence, climatic conditions, progress made within the program, and the institutional and policy environment for building disaster and climate resilience.

Outputs of the analysis stage

- A document developed in consultation with stakeholders that describes the method and results obtained, which is shared with the target population in an accessible language
- A context analysis and baseline comprised of key data selected from the overall results
- An initial assessment report on disaster and climate change risk that identifies the key priorities agreed by all stakeholders, (particularly the target population), and those for which stakeholders are best placed to respond

Tools and resources

For information and links, see *Tools and resources* p.139.

3.3 Design

The purpose of the design stage is to use the findings of the analysis to develop a program, or new strategies within an existing program, that will build disaster and climate resilience within the target population. During the design process, the program's goal and objectives should be defined, as well as the results it will seek to achieve, and the activities to be carried out.

Ideally, design should immediately follow analysis, to build on interest and awareness raised among stakeholders.

The design of a disaster risk reduction and climate change adaptation intervention will depend on:

- The issues raised during the analysis.
- The responsibility, priorities and competencies of the organization planning to carry out the program.
- Other programs and plans in the area that may be complementary, and how program design would add to, not duplicate, other programs.
- Potential partners, allies and networks.
- Available funding and funding restrictions.

Within these parameters, the design of a disaster risk reduction and climate change adaptation program at the local level is likely to include strategies to:

- Strengthen at-risk populations' and other stakeholders' access to, and understanding of, current and future risks[G], their ability to assess them, and their capacity to make appropriate choices to manage them. For example, public information campaigns, hazard mapping and monitoring, improving access to meteorological forecasting, and effective early warning systems[G], as well as exercises/'games' to support understanding and appropriate application of climate information and the levels of certainty within it.
- Develop or reinforce structures, mechanisms and resources to prepare for, respond to, and facilitate recovery from hazards and high-impact changes. For example, disaster management committees, emergency services, contingency plans, contingency funds, social insurance, grain banks, and temporary shelters.
- Build a diverse asset base to strengthen livelihoods and wellbeing, and to manage risk. For example, multiple income sources and livelihood options, household savings, sustainable natural resources (such as water sources, fertile land, forests), good health, and social networks.
- Protect assets and services from current and projected hazards and climate conditions. For example, hazard-resilient building techniques for homes,

schools and hospitals; and appropriate technology for water distribution and sanitation systems.

- Reduce risk by advancing locally appropriate adaptation technologies. For example, the use of drought-tolerant seed varieties, improved grain storage, and water harvesting.

- Protect the environment. For example, integrated watershed management practices, erosion control, and reforestation.

At national levels, disaster risk reduction and climate change adaptation programming is likely to include strategies to:

- Strengthen institutions and entitlement systems to ensure equitable access to key assets for resilience and adaptation. For example, national policies on access to potable water, health services, education, climate information and other basic rights; local norms that regulate access to natural resources; laws that respect ancestral land rights of indigenous groups; and social customs that encourage wealthier households to support poorer neighbors in times of stress[G] or crisis.

- Support people's ability to influence policy and planning processes at different levels of government and governance[G] processes. For example, through popular campaigning activities which provide opportunities for at-risk populations to raise concerns about disaster and climate risk that are heard and acted upon by decision makers.

- Support people's ability to innovate and learn from innovation. For example, provide inputs or insurance for changing crop types, provide training in new employment skills, promote up-take of improved sanitation designs, etc.

- Establish or strengthen governance frameworks for managing disaster and climate change risk, such as national laws, dedicated ministries and mainstreaming[G] policies, and mechanisms to involve multiple stakeholders and levels in decision-making so that efforts can be scaled up from local to district and national levels.

- Develop longer-term plans and responses to disasters and climate change that: 1) are inclusive of multiple departments and ministries in a 'whole of government' approach; 2) identify key partnerships from different sectors of society to develop and implement specific projects; and 3) identify human and financial resources required to fully fund plans and responses.

Further details about sector-specific disaster risk reduction and climate change adaptation programming can be found in *Chapter 4: Key sectors, disaster risk reduction and climate change adaptation.*

Key steps in the design stage

There are five key steps in the design stage:

1. *Define the design process and program scope*:

   - Agree among the main stakeholders how the design process should be undertaken, by whom, and what expertise is needed.

   - If time has passed since the analysis stage, check the contextual baseline, identify any new sources of information, and update the analysis.

   - Discuss the key issues generated by the analysis, the responsibilities and competences of the implementing organization(s), the focus of other programs and plans in the area, and the likely amounts and conditions of funding.

   - Decide the interventions, duration, and the communities or populations that the program intends to benefit.

2. *Develop the program logic*:

   - Define, or in the case of an existing program, verify and redefine the program's objectives. For specific disaster risk reduction and climate change adaptation programs, objectives are likely to specifically refer to building disaster and climate resilience. Objectives of programs in which disaster risk reduction and climate change adaptation measures are being integrated are likely to be broader, but should refer to the sustainability of program impacts in a context of disaster and climate change risk.

   - Develop corresponding activities to achieve the objectives, outputs and overall impact goal. These should build on the most effective and sustainable strategies already being used by at-risk populations to manage risk and draw upon the expertise available within the implementing agency or include a budget to ensure that appropriate expertise is part of the project.

   - Include contingency measures to respond to hazards and effects of climate change that may occur during the project's lifetime.

   - State the assumptions on which the program is based, and make explicit the need for flexibility to adapt it to any unforeseen or uncertain aspects of climate change.

3. *Develop an advocacy plan*:

   - Decide which factors are key to creating an enabling environment for the program and other disaster risk reduction and climate change adaptation efforts, using the information generated during the analysis stage on relevant institutions, policies and other actors. For example, the approval of a national climate change policy, or legislation requiring all levels of government to make budget allocations for disaster risk reduction may be critical for generating a cooperative relationship with local government.

- Initiate further research, if necessary, to gain a better understanding of how particular factors may be influenced.

- Modify the program logic if necessary, to reflect the components of the advocacy plan.

- For more guidance on advocacy, see *Chapter 6: Creating an enabling environment for disaster risk reduction and climate change adaptation.*

4. *Create a monitoring framework and knowledge management plan:*

- Discuss and agree among stakeholders what kinds of indicators are most appropriate for monitoring the program's progress. Make use of recent participatory research on the characteristics of resilience, as well as other resources mentioned below to support the discussion. As with all programs, ensure the indicators selected are SMART (**S**pecific, **M**easurable, **A**chievable in a cost effective way, **R**elevant for the program, and available in a **T**imely manner) and gender-specific where relevant.

- Refine the relevant aspects of the baseline created in the analysis stage to document the pre-program situation in relation to the indicators selected.

- Create a plan for collecting and analyzing monitoring data in relation to the program baseline and the external baseline. It is very important to monitor both, as changes in the external context usually require program modifications.

- Identify potential areas of learning that may be useful for others, such as innovative technology, contextual challenges, etc, and define how knowledge generated on these issues will be captured and shared. Add specific activities within the program logic to cater to this.

- Discuss and agree among stakeholders what kind of evaluation(s) should take place. For longer-term or highly innovative programs, a mid-term evaluation may be useful in addition to a final evaluation.[26]

5. *Draw up the program budget:*

- Define the human, financial and material resources needed to carry out and monitor the proposed activities (including those for advocacy).

- Within the human resource budget line, include an item for staff capacity building, as it is likely that staff will need to develop knowledge or skills specific to disaster risk reduction and climate change adaptation.

- Include contingency funds for responding to hazards or effects of climate change during the program's lifetime.

- Wherever possible, build flexibility into the budget to allow for changes during implementation. The uncertainty of climate change projections, and the innovative nature of some resilience-building actions mean that programs and budgets may require significant changes. This should also include community in-kind contributions to the program.

Outputs of the design stage

- Program outline
- Advocacy plan
- Program-specific baseline
- Monitoring framework including a beneficiary accountability plan/system
- Indicators of change document
- Knowledge management plan

CASE STUDY: POST-CYCLONE RECONSTRUCTION AND REHABILITATION PROJECT

Madagascar, CARE International

Madagascar, one of the world's 30 poorest nations, is regularly hit by cyclones, several of which have been very violent and affected most of the country. Although people are familiar with cyclones and their consequences, local authorities have few resources to prepare for future hazards.

In Antalaha district in the northeast, people often live on river banks or in coastal villages. This provides canoe and water accessibility, limiting dependability on other transport, but also directly exposes people to the effects of cyclones. In the past 12 years, Antalaha has been hit eight times by cyclones, three of which were classified as high-intensity tropical cyclones.

Following the storm surges resulting from cyclones, erosion in coastal areas has increased and, in some villages, the sea front has advanced more than 100 meters resulting in the loss of more than 50 percent of village land and main roads. Erosion has been amplified by the loss of coastal trees, which acted as windbreakers, and destruction of mangroves and coral reefs, which before had reduced the impact of storm surges.

The analysis stage of the program cycle considered the level of destruction by cyclones between 2000 and 2004—which had resulted in the destruction of two bridges (of 45 meters and 100 meters) and a ferry—to determine how best to rebuild community infrastructure. CARE concluded that, rather than repeatedly repairing the bridges, it would be more effective to invite the 2,000 people in the communities of Ambodipont and Antsiribe to build a five-kilometer detour further inland. This would involve the community in its own reconstruction effort and would reduce the long-term costs of maintenance since the road would be less exposed to cyclones, storm surges, and erosion. The idea was presented to the village and, after an internal consultation, the villagers decided to construct the detour.

In the second stage of the PCM, the community identified those who could offer their land and/or trees for the construction, and key figures from the villages helped with the negotiations to compensate these households so that the CARE project could be fully designed and implemented with community participation.

Based on the community's decision, the road project was designed to facilitate transportation of people and their goods using food-for-work in the first phase and cash-for-work in the second phase to: (1) Assure the food security of those most affected by cyclones, (2) Facilitate the circulation of people and goods to help restart the local economy (market access), and (3) Improve security and access of the five coastal villages.

By **strengthening the participation of, and action by, the population at risk**, the community took its own decision to build the detour. Not only did the intervention reduce the road's exposure to disasters, but also the population's exposure. Eight years after the construction of the detour, 2,200 coastal inhabitants relocated about one kilometer inland to be closer to the road. They continue to benefit from the economic advantages and access to communication that it provides. By moving further inland, the human impact on the coastal environment has decreased. The distance from villages to agricultural lands was reduced which resulted in increased agricultural production, and the men, who before had spent all of their time at sea or taking care of their fishing materials, were now spending time on agricultural activities with the women.

Tools and resources

For information and links, see *Tools and resources* p.141.

3.4 Implementation

The implementation stage is where planned activities take place, results are generated, and the program is monitored and modified in response to any new conditions or unforeseen situations.

The *purpose* of this stage is to achieve the program's objectives within the planned time period and within the project budget. Implementation encompasses all direct assistance, support, capacity building, advocacy and knowledge management activities.

Key steps in the implementation stage

There are three key steps at the start of this phase (start-up activities), and three areas that require constant attention:

Start-up activities

1. *Produce an operational plan in conjunction with the target community and other stakeholders:*
   - Draw up a realistic schedule for starting and completing all the program's planned activities and share it with all relevant parties.
   - As far as possible, allow flexibility to prepare for and respond to any hazards that may occur during the program's lifetime, particularly in contexts of recurrent hazards, such as flooding during monsoon seasons.

2. *Confirm partnerships and networks:*
   - Meet with partners and allies to further develop program plans, adapt where necessary (if the context has changed) and coordinate activities.
   - Discuss and formalize agreements on roles and responsibilities for implementation, and advocacy and knowledge management with partners and allies.

3. *Develop capacity of staff and partners:*
   - Using information gathered in the analysis stage, develop a suitable capacity development plan in accordance with the program needs and any gaps identified, and incorporate it into the main program plan to ensure that it is resourced and implemented.

Areas for constant attention during implementation

1. *Monitoring, evaluation and learning, and knowledge management*:
   - Ensure that the program's activities, outputs and outcomes, as well as the external context are systematically monitored in accordance with the monitoring plan, analyzed, and that the results are shared with all stakeholders, so that the program can be refined in its design and improved for its ongoing implementation.

- Ensure that relevant data is disaggregated by gender[G] and other differential factors.
- Be aware of unforeseen impacts, particularly negative ones, and make changes to the program if necessary.
- Produce and share examples of innovative or successful practice.
- Plan for, and carry out, learning reviews and evaluations at key intervals as part of the ongoing program cycle.

2. *Participation of high- risk groups*:

- Check that the program is meeting the practical and strategic needs of women, men, and children, and of high-risk groups; if not, use their input to make modifications, and check again.
- Capture specific lessons about gender and diversity in disaster risk reduction and climate change adaptation programming, to promote uptake of good practice.

3. *Emergency preparedness and response*:

- Draw up a contingency or disaster preparedness[G] plan with all stakeholders at the start of the implementation stage of the program, and revise it at regular intervals during the program.
- Reinforce or establish a basic early warning system for all relevant hazards and climate conditions at the start of the implementation stage, then test and enhance it periodically as the program progresses.
- Ensure all actors (target populations, program staff and those of other organizations) are aware of their roles, responsibilities and procedures for emergency response; test them regularly through organized simulation and informal checks, to develop a culture of preparedness.

Tools and resources

For information and links, see *Tools and resources* p.142.

Guidance for applying the 10 principles for integrated disaster risk reduction and climate change adaptation in program cycle management	
1. Increase understanding of the hazard and climate change context.	• Gather information from a variety of primary and secondary sources in order to gain an overall understanding of the context. • Keep in mind that climate data and projections at sub-national and local scales do not exist for many developing countries, so use broad trends and scenarios from the best available data.

Guidance for applying the 10 principles for integrated disaster risk reduction and climate change adaptation in program cycle management

2. Increase understanding of exposure, vulnerability and capacity.	• Actively engage all stakeholders in the analysis stage, to build their capacity to understand and assess risk as a direct result of their involvement in the process. • Monitor the external baseline during the design stage, and update the analysis if necessary.
3. Recognize rights and responsibilities.	• Disaggregate information gathered by sex, age and other relevant social, cultural and economic factors to understand the particular needs of different groups. • Report back to stakeholders and maintain accountability throughout the design process.
4. Strengthen participation of, and action, by the population at risk.	• Use a participatory data collection analysis process with target populations. This method of action-research generates awareness of risk, facilitates active involvement of different groups and ownership of future action. • Document the program design process, including the rationale behind key decisions and how stakeholders were involved, to facilitate program implementation and learning, and the involvement of different groups. • Plan around stakeholders' commitments, restrictions and peak work periods, such as factory shifts, commuting times, harvests, and tropical storm seasons, so that at-risk populations may engage fully in the program when their input is required, and to ensure that interventions are implemented at the appropriate times to be effective.
5. Promote systemic engagement and change.	• Provide opportunities for cross-program learning for staff, participants and partners given the new concepts and information about climate change, and the need for a joint approach between disaster risk reduction and climate change adaptation. • Encourage multi-stakeholder reviews and evaluations to generate discussion between different stakeholders.
6. Foster synergy between multiple levels.	• Ensure that the stages of PCM address different levels of intervention from local level to district, provincial and national. Without an enabling political and institutional environment, a program's achievements are likely to be limited or unsustainable. • Use institutional strengthening and civil society[G] capacity-building components in programs to facilitate dialogue and coordination between stakeholders at different levels.

Guidance for applying the 10 principles for integrated disaster risk reduction and climate change adaptation in program cycle management	
7. Draw on and build diverse sources of knowledge.	• Use as many sources of information as possible but do not be put off if external sources on the target location are not available; just work with the data that the local-level analysis generates. • Work with government department(s) responsible for disaster risk reduction and climate change adaptation where they exist, as well as other departments with responsibility for food security, livelihoods, water, education, health, housing, protection[G], etc. • Seek input from technical experts (such as climate scientists, gender and diversity experts, agronomists, water engineers, economists, etc.) for relevant parts of the program design and when conducting evaluations.
8. Instill flexibility and responsiveness.	• Recognize that data collection should not focus on one type of hazard or one set of climate conditions. Climate change is causing variations to the types of hazards experienced around the world, so a multi-hazard, multiple-scenario approach is important. • Be prepared for uncertainty in climate data, and reflect this in any outputs produced during the different PCM stages. • Be prepared for situations that require changes to the operational plan. Uncertainty in climate change projections and the unpredictable nature of many hazards mean that programs may need multiple adjustments in response to the changing external context. • Evaluate the program after a major hazard or each relevant risk period to see what worked, what did not, and what needs to change.
9. Address different timescales.	• Consider future climate projections and changing hazard profiles, as well as current ones, when undertaking the analysis stage. • Ensure that the program design includes components to deal with current and future risk. • Continue to monitor variables in the contextual baseline that may affect program success throughout the implementation stage.
10. Do no harm.	• Incorporate a conflict-sensitive approach into local-level analysis in contexts of open or latent conflict[G] (for more guidance, refer to *Chapter 5: Key contexts*). • Track both the intended and unintended impacts of program activities to ensure that any negative impacts can be avoided or addressed. • Share mistakes as well as good practice and successes, to scale-up learning from particular approaches, technology and methodologies.

4

KEY SECTORS
FOR DISASTER RISK REDUCTION
AND CLIMATE CHANGE ADAPTATION

Chapter 4 is designed to help development and humanitarian practitioners understand how disasters[G] and climate change[G] impact key sectors in development and humanitarian settings, and provides guidance on how to program in these areas. It includes:

- *Explanations* of:
  - Key terms, basic concepts and approaches relevant to key sectors.

  - Key issues in relation to disaster and climate change risk and the key sectors of food security; livelihoods[G]; natural resource management[G]; water, sanitation and hygiene (WASH); education; health; and protection.[27]

- *Guidelines* for applying an integrated approach to disaster risk reduction[G] and climate change adaptation[G] to different sectoral interventions, including application of the 10 principles.

- *Case studies* of disaster risk reduction, climate change adaptation and key sectors in practice.

- Links to *Tools and resources* to implement disaster risk reduction and climate change adaptation in key sectors.

4.1 Food security

'*Food security exists when all people at all times have physical or economic access to sufficient, safe and nutritious food to meet their dietary needs and food preferences for an active and healthy life.*'[28]

Governments are legally bound to ensure the right to food for all. Yet, despite a planet with sufficient food, the global food system fails to provide adequate nutrition and calories to everyone; over one billion people remain hungry and millions more are food insecure.[29] As the global population grows to about nine billion by 2050, the food system faces additional pressure, compounded by climate change[G], disasters[G], and the negative impacts of agricultural subsidies, speculation, price volatility and other issues.[30,31]

Food insecurity[G] impacts poverty-affected populations not only in terms of their health, but also their livelihoods[G] through the depletion of natural resources, and it causes people to sell assets, migrate in order to find work, and take other measures to survive. With growing urban populations, implications for land use and other natural resource uses, food production systems, and access to food become ever more important considerations.[32]

This section should be read alongside the *Livelihoods* and *Natural resource management* sections below given their inherent links.

Key issues

The impacts of disasters and climate change on food security are numerous. Shifting weather patterns and extreme weather will increase the incidence of droughts and floods, heat waves, frost and other extreme events affecting all four key dimensions of food security: availability, access, stability and utilization.[33]

Box 4.1: Example impacts of disasters and climate change on the four dimensions of food security

- **Availability**: Reduced harvests or death of livestock from severe drought; shortage of seeds leading to reduced yields.

- **Access**: Damaged infrastructure cutting off access to food or markets; low livestock prices causing a reduction in cash availability to buy food.

- **Stabilization**: Unpredictable weather patterns affecting yields of certain crops or the regular planting of staple foods.

- **Utilisation**: Unsafe drinking water that causes chronic diarrhea resulting in decreased absorption of nutrients.

Source: Adapted from IFRC (2006) How to conduct a food security assessment: a step-by-step guide for National Societies in Africa. *Geneva, Switzerland.*

With climate change impacts on agricultural production worldwide, areas suffering from food insecurity are expected to experience disproportionately negative effects.[34] Already fragile food production systems and the natural resources on which they depend, particularly those prone to degradation, desertification[G] and water stress[G], will undermine the capacity[G] of people to take the needed preventative and protective measures.[35] Rain-fed agriculture[G] and agro-pastoral systems are at particular risk.

Disaster-affected communities that suffer chronic and transient food insecurity may also become acutely food insecure during disaster events. A lack of food or not being able to afford or access food is one of the major impacts of disasters.[36]

Rates of acute and chronic malnutrition are also expected to rise due to increased crop failure, decreased fish stocks, and diarrheal disease caused by poor water quality. The nutritional status of the world's poorest people, whose livelihoods depend on climate-sensitive resources, will be deeply affected by changes in the climate. In addition, their poor nutrition will impact on their health and ability to work, and will hinder their capacity to adapt.

Taking an approach to food security that incorporates disaster risk reduction[G] and climate change adaptation will increase the resilience[G] of at-risk populations to disaster and climate change risk, at the same time protecting and enhancing local ecosystems and enhancing human resources needed to reduce overall vulnerability[G].

Guidance for applying the 10 principles for integrated disaster risk reduction and climate change adaptation in food security	
1. Increase understanding of the hazard and climate change context.	• Conduct agricultural assessments to better understand the current and predicted impacts of hazards, climate variability and change. • Support the development of climate and disaster risk profile maps and actions plans at local, district and provincial levels. • Support the creation of district and village level information hubs where communities can access information, education and communication (IEC) materials, local forecasts and disaster and climate hazard profile maps.
2. Increase understanding of exposure, vulnerability and capacity.	• Use the best available information on hazards, climate change trends and land/natural resource use to identify the degree to which food sources, mechanisms for accessing food (including productive assets and employment in other industries), and relevant infrastructure (such as roads connecting producers, consumers and markets, and food processing plants) are exposed. • Conduct participatory capacity and vulnerability analysis[G] (PCVA) at local levels to help at-risk populations better understand the linkages between their food security and disaster and climate change risk; ensure that the gender[G] dimensions of food security, vulnerability and capacities are identified and understood by participating men and women. • Use methodologies such as the Household Economy Approach (See *Tools and resources* p.152) to deepen understanding of the range of factors that affect the at-risk population's food security and nutrition (such as seasonality, remittances, staple food prices and conflict) and how these interact with disaster and climate change risk. • Increase at-risk populations' awareness of the central role of women in the food system via education and training.[37]

Guidance for applying the 10 principles for integrated disaster risk reduction and climate change adaptation in food security	
3. Recognize rights and responsibilities.	• Raise the profile of disaster and climate change risks for food security through public awareness campaigns, lobbying of relevant government stakeholders[G] and advocacy to key international donors/funders, to increase demand for climate-smart investment in, and governance[G] of, food security. • Use popular media, traditional communications channels and direct capacity building to increase household-level understanding of the links between climate change, natural resource management[G] and food security, and provide information on responsible management of natural resources. • Advocate for the realization of women's and marginalized people's rights to critical livelihood resources such as land and water through public awareness campaigns, legislative reform and direct support to civil society[G] and community-based organizations working on these issues.
4. Strengthen participation of, and action by, population at risk.	• Support the creation/strengthening of mechanisms (such as radio broadcasts and text messaging) by which local climate forecasts and hazard updates can be disseminated. • Support market information systems (price, quality standards, products) at district and local levels to enable food producers and purchasers to take informed decisions. • Work with food producers at high risk (particularly women and marginalized populations) to increase productivity by strengthening land and water rights, increasing access to markets, finance and insurance.[38] • Provide training and peer-to-peer education to farmers on conservation agriculture[G] practices, restoration of degraded soils and agricultural biodiversity[G] within communities. • Establish food and nutrition groups in at-risk communities and provide training on household-level strategies for improving and safeguarding nutrition in a changing climate and as disaster preparedness[G] measures.
5. Foster systemic engagement and change.	• Advocate for food security, health, agriculture and economic development policies to be based on analysis of disaster and climate change risk.

Guidance for applying the 10 principles for integrated disaster risk reduction and climate change adaptation in food security	
5. Foster systemic engagement and change.	• Advocate for investment in effective social protection[G] systems that can be scaled up in anticipation of increased food insecurity (including as a result of climate-induced stresses[G]) and in response to crises; where appropriate, support pilot projects to trial measures such as cash transfers, food vouchers and guaranteed labor schemes. • Promote coordination between non-governmental organizations working on food security, livelihoods, health and WASH, in areas of chronic food insecurity, to generate holistic, longer-term strategies for disaster and climate change resilience.
6. Foster synergy between multiple levels.	• Identify national laws and policies relevant to food security, climate change and disaster risk[G], and support at-risk populations to advocate for their implementation. • Support the development of multi-level food security monitoring and contingency planning[G] using systems such as the Integrated Food Security Phase Classification (IPC) tool (See *Tools and resources* p.143). • See section *5.4 Slow-onset disasters*.
7. Draw on and build diverse sources of knowledge.	• Support the development of systems that improve food producers' access to climate information on a range of timescales, from days (weather), months (seasonal outlooks) to decades (climate change scenarios). • Organize local to national platforms for food producers, food security specialists and disaster and climate change experts, to generate shared understanding of the challenges and collaboration in generating solutions. • Establish pilot projects linking small and medium-scale producers, suppliers of technology, and scientific institutions, to encourage innovation. • Encourage at-risk populations to identify traditional food security practices such as seed and grain banks, conservation, savings schemes, migration and seasonal labor, and assess how they may be relevant for, or adapted to, future climate scenarios.
8. Instill flexibility and responsiveness.	• Work with different levels of government to develop contingency food reserves and funds for early action in situations of growing food insecurity due to hazard events or climate-related stresses. • Support local and regional government institutions to access and act upon information generated using the IPC tool and, where possible, to contribute to its generation.

Guidance for applying the 10 principles for integrated disaster risk reduction and climate change adaptation in food security	
9. Address different timescales.	• Include early warning indicators for food insecurity in program monitoring systems, and put in place mechanisms for moving to early action, such as contingency supplies/funding. • Support households and communities to take preparedness measures such as food and fodder storage, animal vaccine campaigns, savings and micro-insurance. • Support the development of context-specific research into food security over different timescales to support better planning for, and responses to, changing disaster and climate risk. • Assess the relevance of national food security policy and strategies for current and future risk scenarios; identify potential strengths, weaknesses and gaps, and advocate for the development of policy and strategies that takes into account climate change projections. • Assist at-risk populations to understand and access micro-insurance schemes.
10. Do no harm.	• Analyze the potential impact on prices for local producers and local markets when providing food or non-food items during emergency responses. • Consider cash-for-work and cash transfer programming as a means to protect food insecure populations while also supporting local food producers and suppliers.

Box 4.2: Food security measures

Achieving food security for all in light of the impacts of climate change and disasters requires a coordinated effort that incorporates preventive, promotional, protective and transformative measures.

1. **Preventive measures that support people to avoid food insecurity**: For example, social safety net systems such as credit and savings groups, as well as risk-management measures such as crop diversification and drought cycle management.

2. **Promotional measures that aim to reduce vulnerability to food insecurity by enhancing incomes and capacities**: For example, better access to markets and livelihoods diversification; better information about climate projections; data collection for weather, land use, crops and livestock; and financial services including savings, credit and insurance.

3. **Protective actions that act as relief measures, required when preventive and promotional measures fail**: For example, food-for-work and cash-for-work programs.

4. **Transformative measures that seek to address issues of social inequity and exclusion**: For example, ensuring women are central to the development of farmer's cooperatives and saving schemes. Transformative measures underpin the first three measures.

Source: Adapted from Devereux, S. and Sabates-Wheeler, R. (2004) Transformative Social Protection. *IDS Working Paper 232. (The order has been changed to reflect the need to focus on preventive and promotional measures, with protective measures needed when these fail.)*

CASE STUDY: ALTERNATIVE LIVELIHOODS FOR VULNERABLE RIVERSIDE COMMUNITIES[39]

Ghana, World Vision International

In Ghana's Talensi Nabdam district, three communities—Yinduri, Pwalugu and Santeng—along the White Volta river in the northeast of the country repeatedly experience drought, floods, wild fire, and disease. People in these riverside communities earn their livelihoods by cultivating along the river bank that provides the only available productive land, while the rest of the land is rocky and unproductive.

During torrential rains, a hydro-electric power dam in neighboring Burkina Faso overflows, resulting in serious flooding in northern Ghana and leading to damage of crops, homes and even loss of lives. In 2009, the three communities were seriously affected by flooding along more than 25km of the river bank. Farmers' fields, which were predominantly maize, were washed away, leaving little or no harvest.

Climate change is affecting Ghana's population by disrupting agricultural systems, flooding coastal areas and lowering water levels around the Volta River delta which provides around 80 percent of Ghana's electric supply.[40] Climate change is projected to have significant impacts on Ghana. Although there will be fluctuations in both annual temperatures and precipitation, the trend for temperature over the period 2010–50 indicates warming in all regions.

World Vision International's Regional Community Resilience Program enabled households and communities to diversify their income sources, increase crop yields, manage natural resources sustainably and protect livelihoods against adverse effects or shocks[G] for long-term disaster risk reduction.

As part of World Vision's integrated approach to disaster risk reduction and capacity building, farmers found opportunity in the flood water for alternative livelihoods that made use of residual moisture in the soil. After the flood waters receded, they planted suitable short-maturing crops such as watermelon, yellow melon and beans, which they were able to consume or sell for income generation. By **instilling flexibility and responsiveness** with a longer-term focus, the integrated project had the multiple benefits of (a) enhancing household income and productivity through the sale of agricultural products, (b) equipping farmers with new livelihoods knowledge and skills, (c) adapting agricultural practices that are more resilient to the shocks and stresses of that environment, and (d) enhancing the nutritional status of household members through the increased consumption of nutritious foods.

Lessons learnt during the project showed that: (a) There should be support for households and communities to employ different strategies and to innovate to ensure sufficient access to, and provision of, food throughout the year, income for regular needs, and savings for times of emergency particularly given the impacts of climate change in the region; and (b) possible future scenarios should be taken into consideration when planning livelihoods options, including the possible outcomes of future trends such as climate change, globalisation, migration and environmental degradation. Being able to prepare and adapt is a key factor in effectively responding to dynamic change over the long term.

Tools and resources

For information and links, see *Tools and resources* p.143.

4.2 Livelihoods

A livelihood[G] comprises the resources (including skills, technology and organizations) and activities required to make a living and have a good quality of life.[41] Understanding livelihoods requires looking beyond a person's main source of employment or income, to include all the activities and choices within the household and local population that provide food, health, income, shelter and other tangible and intangible benefits, such as comfort, safety, respect and fulfillment.[42]

The lives, production, assets, and income of women and men engaged in subsistence, market-based livelihoods and waged employment are increasingly exposed to the risks[G] of natural hazards[G] and climate change, exacerbating risks already experienced from globalization of the economy, gender[G], migration and other inequalities.

This section should be read alongside the *Food security* and *Natural resource management* sections given their inherent links.

Box 4.3: Examples of livelihood activities

- Agricultural production (crops, vegetables, livestock, fish) for home consumption or for sale.
- Non-agricultural home production (tailoring, pottery, food processing, etc).
- Waged employment (local or through migration to other areas).
- Harvesting forest products (for fuel and firewood, food, or non-timber forest products, etc.).

Source: Pasteur, K. (2011) From Vulnerability to Resilience: A framework for analysis and action to build community resilience, *Rugby, UK: Practical Action Publishing*

Key issues

Many livelihoods are exposed to hazards that may become, or escalate into, a disaster[G] when the capacity[G] of at-risk populations is low. Examples of hazards include: droughts and floods, poorly planned infrastructure, conflict[G], earthquakes, pest infestation, market failure, and increases in food prices. Even small shocks[G] that are not necessarily considered disasters (and therefore do not receive humanitarian relief) can have a profoundly negative effect on at-risk populations, especially when they re-occur over numerous years. When combined with stresses brought about by climate change (such as rainfall variability), this can make it harder for communities to recover from a shock, and find them oscillating between emergency and recovery, eroding resilience[G] over time.

The impacts of hazards and climate change effects[G] can cause:

- Sudden, possibly temporary, loss of access to one or more key assets/resources;
- Undermining of the sustainability of current agriculture-dependent rural livelihoods and urban livelihoods that depend on rural supply chains;
- Stress on already depleted natural resources; and
- Increasing frequency and intensity of hazards that can lead to climate-related disasters.

Box 4.4: Examples of expected future climate change impacts on agriculture

- Decreased yield of major cereals in dry and tropical regions, even with slight warming.
- Increased irrigation demand, coupled with declines in water availability in some regions due to decreases in rainfall in the subtropics (particularly affecting rain-fed agriculture in Central America and sub-tropical Africa) and in other regions due to snow and glacial melt.
- Reduced productivity and fertility of animals due to heat and water stress.
- Extinction of some local fish species as a result of ocean warming and acidification.
- Increases in extreme rainfall in production areas.
- Inundation of crop lands by saline water in low-lying coastal areas.

Source: Pettengell, C. (2010) Climate Change Adaptation: Enabling people living in poverty to adapt. *Oxford, UK: Oxfam International*

Rural livelihoods that are principally dependent on rain-fed agriculture[G] are particularly vulnerable because their activities are by nature climate sensitive. While at-risk populations have considerable experience in dealing with climate variability[G] and recurrent disasters, and have generations of context-specific knowledge, increasing disaster and climate change risk is now taking them beyond traditional 'coping' strategies, into unchartered territory, where new knowledge and practice may be needed.[43]

Reduced productivity in rural livelihoods also affects the many urban livelihoods that depend on inputs from rural areas. Disasters in rural areas can lead to migration and increased urbanization, increasing populations beyond the absorptive capacity of industries, thereby increasing unemployment. Urban livelihoods can also be directly affected by disasters and climate change, which can destroy assets and infrastructure (such as roads and bridges, severing access to markets), reduce economic liquidity, and make financial services inaccessible.

A Sustainable Livelihoods Approach (SLA) is an accepted method for improving understanding of livelihoods and supporting people to build their capacity and resilience in the face of disaster and climate change risk.[44] It draws on the main factors that affect people's livelihoods and the typical relationships between these factors. It can be used in planning new development activities and in assessing the contribution that existing activities have made to sustaining livelihoods.

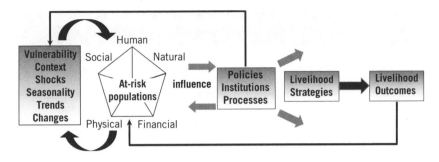

Figure 4.1: Sustainable Livelihoods Approach (SLA)
Source: IFAD (n.d.) The Sustainable Livelihoods Approach [online] http://www.ifad.org/sla/index.htm

The SLA places people at the centre of a web of inter-related influences that affect how they create a livelihood for themselves and their households. Closest to those at the centre are the resources and livelihood assets they have access to and use of. These can include natural resources; technology; their skills, knowledge and capacity; their health; access to education; sources of credit; and their networks of social support. The extent of their access to these assets is strongly influenced by their vulnerability[G] context, which takes account of trends (e.g. economic, political, and technological); shocks (e.g. epidemics, natural disasters, civil strife); and seasonality (e.g. prices, production, and employment opportunities). Access is also influenced by the prevailing social, institutional and political environment, which affects the ways in which people combine and use their assets to achieve their goals. These are their livelihood strategies. For more information on a SLA, see *Tools and resources* p.144.

Guidance for applying the 10 principles for integrated disaster risk reduction and climate change adaptation in livelihoods	
1. Increase understanding of the hazard and climate change context.	• Compile information on known hazards and the projected effects of climate change on the program location and the wider geographical context (including production/manufacturing areas, commercial centers, supply and distribution chains, and markets) on which the target population's livelihoods depend.
2. Increase understanding of exposure, vulnerability and capacity.	• Assess to what extent assets in the value chains of the target population's livelihoods are exposed to identified hazards and effects of climate change.

Guidance for applying the 10 principles for integrated disaster risk reduction and climate change adaptation in livelihoods	
2. Increase understanding of exposure, vulnerability and capacity.	• Use participatory capacity and vulnerability analysis with different livelihoods groups within the target population and other stakeholders to understand the extent to which exposed assets—including all the people engaged in the livelihoods strategies—are vulnerable (e.g. unvaccinated livestock, unprotected water sources, workers living in poorly constructed housing, etc.). • Identify existing capacities relevant to the target population's livelihoods (including knowledge, skills, organizations and networks, as well as physical and economic assets) and how these might be developed to build resilience.
3. Recognize rights and responsibilities.	• Support at-risk populations to understand how the right to a livelihood and other related rights are reflected in national legislation and policies, and which institutions are responsible for implementing it. • Support at-risk populations to secure equitable access to natural resources required for their livelihoods, and to realize their rights to safe housing as a key factor in human health and component of many livelihoods strategies (for production, storage of equipment, stock and produce, and trade). • Advocate for construction and workplace safety standards to be put in place and adhered to. • Train staff to understand how gender and other marginalized statuses can interact with livelihoods opportunities, and ensure that all actions and interventions promote equity.
4 Strengthen participation of, and action by, population at risk.	• Develop audience-appropriate materials and methods to build the capacity of livelihoods-oriented organizations such as producers' associations and trade unions, to improve their understanding of disaster and climate change risk and how it affects their livelihoods. • Support the creation/strengthening of mechanisms (such as radio broadcasts and text messaging) by which local climate forecasts and hazard updates can be disseminated. • Support the development of, and access to, market information systems (price, quality standards, products) at district and local levels to enable producers and suppliers to take informed decisions; take care to ensure that women's and men's information needs are met by the systems through adequate consultation and monitoring.

Guidance for applying the 10 principles for integrated disaster risk reduction and climate change adaptation in livelihoods	
4 Strengthen participation of, and action by, population at risk.	• Use participatory methods to support men and women producers to assess the risks and benefits associated with traditional and new techniques/technology options that may help to reduce disaster risk[G] and build resilience to climate change and variability.
5. Promote systemic engagement and change.	• Advocate for economic development policies to be based on analysis of disaster and climate change risk, and for investment in infrastructure and technology to support the development of resilient livelihoods.
	• Engage all relevant government departments/ministries with a role in livelihoods (such as departments of agriculture, labor and transportation) in national platforms and forums for disaster risk reduction and climate change adaptation.
	• Advocate for the involvement of private sector companies in local, district and national risk assessment and contingency planning[G] processes, and for incentives to be made available to them for contributing to disaster and climate change resilience through measures such as retrofitting of workplaces, local hazard mitigation[G] works, and employees loans for housing improvement).
6. Foster synergy between multiple levels.	• Support the participation of representatives of local and district government representatives and grassroots organizations in the development of national policy discussions/revisions.
	• Document processes and lessons learnt in local-level projects promoting livelihoods resilience, to facilitate scale-up of successful initiatives.
7. Draw on and build diverse sources of knowledge.	• Encourage local men, women and children from all livelihoods groups within at-risk populations to share their knowledge and experiences of climate variability and hazard occurrence, to enable communities to identify trends.
	• Encourage older people from all livelihoods groups within at-risk populations to share traditional livelihoods strategies for managing climate variability and recurrent hazards, and support communities to assess how they may be relevant for, or adapted to, future climate scenarios.
	• Engage scientific institutions to work in partnership with at-risk communities to develop/adapt technologies for farming, fishing, forestry and other rural livelihoods; document pilot projects for potential scale-up and replication.

Guidance for applying the 10 principles for integrated disaster risk reduction and climate change adaptation in livelihoods

8. Instill flexibility and responsiveness.	• Provide financial support and technical advice to men and women in at-risk populations to diversify their income sources as a means of managing risk. • Support the development of and access to financial services such as savings schemes and insurance to buffer shocks; provide training to potential users to ensure they understand how they work. • Offer loans/access to credit and technical support for innovation/diversification in livelihoods.
9 Address different timescales.	• Support at-risk populations to protect livelihoods assets from hazards by, for example, providing shelter for animals during floods, or disaster insurance for small businesses. • Use scenario-building techniques with at-risk populations to assess the sustainability of current livelihoods strategies. Provide user-friendly information on other trends, such as globalization, migration, environmental degradation[G] and commodity price volatility to build men and women's capacities to anticipate and respond to dynamic change in the long term. • Use participatory methods to identify suitable early warning signals for different livelihoods groups, and build them into the design of livelihoods projects/programs. • Incorporate contingency funding into livelihoods projects/programs in areas of disaster and climate change risk, to facilitate early action in response to early warning signals.
10. Do no harm.	• Consider the use of cash transfers in slow-onset and rapid-onset disasters, to prevent stress sales of livelihoods assets and other negative coping mechanisms. • Following disasters, conduct Emergency Market Mapping Analysis/Assessment[G] (EMMA) or Market Information and Food Insecurity Response Analysis (MIFIRA) to examine the relationships between food security, aid and markets. • Consider gender and youth implications of livelihoods interventions. Ask questions such as: Are balances shifting that may place a disproportionate burden on one group or another?

CASE STUDY: USING INDIGENOUS KNOWLEDGE TO REDUCE RISKS AND ADAPT TO CLIMATE CHANGE[45]

Bolivia, Oxfam GB

In Bolivia's Amazonian region of Beni, livelihoods are primarily dependent on rain-fed agriculture but production is severely constrained by unpredictable rain patterns, flood/drought cycles and poor soil conditions. Slash-and-burn land practices predominate, whereby the land is productive for only two or three years before new areas of rainforest need to be cleared.

During the rainy season, when water flows into the Amazon tributaries, vital soil nutrients are flushed away due to the detrimental agricultural practices and over use. People are left with sandy soil in which it is difficult to grow crops.

In 2007, Oxfam supported the Kenneth Lee Foundation to revive and adapt an ancient agriculture system of raised, human-made earth platforms to aid improved production during seasonal floods and droughts, reducing losses to common hazards. Drawing on modern scientific understanding of agro-hydrology, with local knowledge, and Oxfam technical support, communities and the municipal authorities constructed a series of 10, raised soil platforms, or *camellones*, 0.5 to 2 meters high, covering an area of about 500 square meters. The platforms

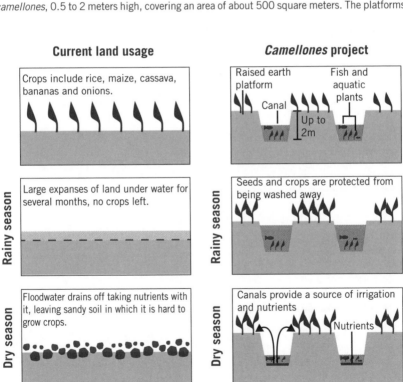

Figure 4.2: Land usage and *camellones*

are surrounded by canals that allow water to flow during the rainy season without flooding the crops and serve as irrigation systems during the dry season. Communities benefited from renewed knowledge from the past, fertile soil, water management systems, organic recycling and animal fodder from production and were able to raise fish in the canals.

Subsequent floods in 2008 in the city of Trinidad, Beni, were the worst floods Bolivia had experienced in 50 years, and affected 118,000 people. Though about 75 percent of the total surface of Beni was flooded, the *camellones* endured. People were able to continue growing a variety of crops for consumption and income generation despite the severe flood situation; improve their household nutrition due to greater soil fertility and better harvests; generate income from selling excess produce at local markets; and reduce the impact on the environment from a reduction in slash-and-burn agricultural practices.

It is not known why this ancient practice vanished but more farmers are now replicating the model, offering a sustainable solution to flood and drought, clearly demonstrating that **drawing on and building diverse sources of knowledge**—ancient indigenous knowledge combined with modern scientific expertise—can produce effective solutions to reduce disaster risks.

Tools and resources

For information and links, see *Tools and resources* p.144.

4.3 Natural resource management

Natural resource management[G] (NRM) is the practice of maintaining and enhancing natural resources such as soil, water, air, minerals, forest, fisheries and flora and fauna through a variety of means, including forest and range management, agroforestry, livestock rearing, water resource management, animal waste management and coastal protection. Recognizing the value of natural resources and ecosystems, prioritizing identification of natural resource concerns and addressing those concerns is critical for ensuring the lives and livelihoods of women, men and children who depend on them.

This section should be read alongside *Food security* and *Livelihoods* sections above, given their inherent links.

Box 4.5: Ecosystem services*

Ecosystem services[G] and their definitions were formalised by the United Nations 2005 Millennium Ecosystem Assessment (MEA) which grouped the services into four broad categories: provisioning, such as the production of food and water; regulating, such as the control of climate and disease; supporting, such as nutrient cycles and crop pollination; and cultural, such as spiritual and recreational benefits. Some examples of ecosystem services include: water filtration, regulation of river flow and groundwater levels, insect pest control, pollination, and maintenance of soil fertility and health. Ecosystem services are not well understood and the important roles of these natural services are not recognized adequately in economic markets, government policies or land management practices. As a result, ecosystems and the services they provide are in decline.**

*Sources: * Millennium Ecosystem Assessment (2005). Ecosystems and Human Well being: A Framework for Assessment. Available at: http://www.maweb.org/documents/ document.48.aspx.pdf*

*** Ecosystem Services Project (n.d.) [online] 'What are ecosystem services'. Available at: http://www.ecosystemservicesproject.org/html/overview/index.htm*

Key issues

Protecting, conserving and enhancing natural resources is not only important for the world's ecosystems; sustainable NRM is vital to maintaining the services required to support the human development of every man, woman and child. Without a healthy planet, the natural resources people need to satisfy their basic needs (such as water, food and shelter) and to achieve a better quality of life would not be available.

There are many examples of the natural environment being degraded or destroyed when environmental protection is sidelined for short-term economic gain, rapid economic growth, or food security needs. Deforestation[G] of native forests and their replacement with commercial oil palm plantations in Indonesia is one example, displacing local communities dependent on forest resources, destroying natural habitats for orangutans, while creating enormous wealth for international companies. Another is the environmental degradation of soils and land in mono-cropping regimes.

Due to the increasing stressors of climate change effects (see Box 4.6), protecting, restoring and enhancing the world's natural resources is now more critical than ever. Disasters[G] and NRM have a complex relationship, as disasters can both exacerbate and be intensified by existing environmental degradation. Not only can natural resource management support adaptation to climate change and buffer communities from some of the worst impacts of climate-related disasters, it can also offer significant opportunities to reduce carbon emissions.

There are, however, many examples of NRM approaches being used as a cost effective and environmentally sound means of reducing risk to climate-related hazards. In Vietnam, planting and protecting 12,000 hectares of mangroves cost approximately $1 million but reduced the costs of sea dyke maintenance by $7.3 million per year.[46]

Box 4.6: The relationship between natural resources, ecosystem services, climate change and disasters

Poor natural resource management

- Landslides due to removal/cutting down of trees.
- Floods caused by silting of rivers provoked by deforestation and soil erosion on crop land.
- Degradation of crop land due to increased rainfall and soil erosion.
- Agricultural drought caused by diversion of water for industrial purposes.
- Agricultural drought as a result of persistent degradation of soils, leading to reduced water-holding capacity and retention rates.
- Mono-cropping and selective agricultural practices that undermine biodiversity.
- Magnification of ecosystem stresses caused by human development (e.g. air and water pollution in urban centers).

Hazard and disaster impacts

- Destruction of crops and removal of top soil due to high winds or water erosion.
- Loss of vegetation due to flooding and excessive saturation of the soil.
- Destruction of wildlife and habitats due to wild fires.
- Degradation of natural resources (forests, water) as a result of large temporary settlements (refugee camps, etc.).

Climate change impacts

- Loss of coral reef, habitats and breeding grounds for fish due to temperature increases.
- Saltwater inundation of land and freshwater sources due to sea-level rise.

> **Box 4.6: The relationship between natural resources, ecosystem services, climate change and disasters (cont.)**
>
> - Loss of biodiversity including massive species extinction due to rising temperatures, loss of habitat, and warming oceans.
> - Loss of forests and grasslands through increasing desertification due to temperature increases, reduction in average annual rainfall.
> - Flooding of urban centres and agricultural areas due to sea-level rise.

The natural resources primarily affected by climate change and other pressures such as environmental degradation, economic growth, and overpopulation include:

Land and soils: Soil fertility is the result of natural processes in healthy ecosystems, which include maintaining forests, vegetative cover, and soil biodiversity[G]. As a result of erosion (caused by wind and water) over the past four decades, 30 percent of the world's arable land has become unproductive. About 60 percent of soil that is eroded ends up in rivers, streams and lakes, making waterways more prone to flooding and to contamination from fertilizers and pesticides.[47] Given that the world's population depends on cropland for food, managing land resources sustainably is vital.[48]

Forests: Grasslands, wetlands, and forests provide resources directly to billions of poor women, men and children, including timber, fuel wood, fiber, medicine and food. Their destruction and degradation —through, for example, logging, construction of large dams, mining and industrial development—continues to take place at a rapid rate; deforestation alone at a rate of 13 million hectares per year.[49]

Water: Water is one of the world's most stressed natural resources due to over-exploitation and competition. By 2030, 47 percent of the world's population will be living in areas of high water stress, and by 2050, the world will require 50 percent more water.[50] Climate change is already creating greater variability in water resources (e.g. more floods and droughts), and this is set to worsen as temperatures rise.

Fisheries: Approximately 75 percent of the world's marine fish stocks are considered either overexploited or fully exploited,[51] due to overfishing and increasing degradation of coastal, marine and freshwater ecosystems and habitats.[52] The ability of the overexploited stocks to recover to sustainable levels from human pressure or from natural disturbances (such as adverse climate conditions, pollution, and disease outbreaks) is now severely compromised.[53] As sea temperatures rise, bringing greater acidification of oceans, fishing stocks will come under further pressure.

Biodiversity: Biodiversity loss occurs gradually and stealthily. Some scientists estimate that the planet is losing 100 species per day as a result of habitat destruction, and that more than a quarter of all species may vanish within the next four decades.[54] Biodiversity conservation (such as the conservation of natural land, freshwater and marine ecosystems and the restoration of degraded ecosystems) is essential because it not only plays a key role in the global carbon cycle and in adapting to climate change, it also provides a wide range of ecosystem services that are essential for human wellbeing.

Box 4.7: Examples of effective natural resource management

- **Sustainable water management**, where river basins, aquifers, flood plains, and their associated vegetation are monitored and managed to provide water storage and flood regulation.

- **Restoration and enhancement of coastal habitats**, such as mangroves, which can be a particularly effective measure against storm surges, saline intrusion, and coastal erosion.

- **Management of grasslands and rangelands** using methods that enhance pastoral livelihoods, increase resilience to drought and flooding, restore lost productivity, and promote sustainability.

- **Establishment of diverse agricultural systems**, where the consideration of local knowledge of specific crop and livestock varieties, maintaining crop and livestock diversity, and conserving diverse agricultural landscapes can help secure food in changing local climatic conditions.

- **Strategic management of shrub lands and forests** to limit the frequency and size of uncontrolled forest fires.

- **Establishment and effective management of protected area systems** to ensure the continued delivery of ecosystem services that increase resilience to climate change.

- **Conservation and restoration of forests** to stabilize land slopes and regulate water flows.

- **Conservation of agro-biodiversity** to provide specific gene pools for crop and livestock adaptation to climate change.

- **Farmer-Managed Natural Regeneration** (the selection and pruning of stems which sprout from indigenous tree and shrub stumps) to increase crop yields, fodder production, and fuel wood availability in degraded dry land areas (particularly successful in West Africa).

- **Community-based forest management** where forests are managed by communities to facilitate sustainable non-timber forest productivity through officially-endorsed and regulated forest management plans. These provide livelihood resources for communities and protect the integrity of the forest canopy, protect biodiversity, regulate the microclimate, and increase carbon capture.

Guidance for applying the 10 principles for integrated disaster risk reduction and climate change adaptation in natural resource management	
1. Increase understanding of the hazard and climate change context.	• Compile information on known hazards and the projected effects of climate change on the program location and the wider geographical context; when defining the scope of the context, take into account that natural resources such as watersheds, forests, groundwater and marine fish stocks may span districts and even country boundaries. • Work with at-risk populations to raise awareness about the importance of natural resources in reducing hazard and climate change risk; their protection[G] and conservation needs, by contextualizing protection, conservation and enhancement approaches already being undertaken for purposes of reducing disaster and climate change risk.
2. Increase understanding of exposure, vulnerability and capacity.	• Support government authorities at different levels to produce and overlay maps of known hazards and the projected effects on climate change on large and small-scale maps of natural resources, to indicate current and potential exposure[G]; and support communities to do the same, at the lowest possible scale. • Use participatory methods with at-risk populations, combined with scientific expertise, to understand the sensitivity of exposed natural resources to the projected effects of climate change. • Use historical disaster records, combined with the knowledge of at-risk populations, to understand the interaction between hazards and natural resources, such as the effects of a volcanic eruption on soil and water. Bear in mind that some natural resources, such as rivers, may also be hazards. • Use participatory methods with at-risk populations to identify how current and traditional practices in the use of natural resources affect exposure and vulnerability to hazards and the projected effects of climate change; use the same methods to identify existing practices, knowledge and skills within at-risk populations for protecting natural resources.
3. Recognize rights and responsibilities.	• Raise awareness among at-risk populations of their right to dispose of natural resources and their related rights to land and food; use audience-appropriate materials to show how these rights are affected by disaster and climate change risk, and the importance of conservation of natural resources in reducing such risks. • Include men, women, adolescents and children in risk assessment processes, to emphasize the role of all members of a community as stewards of the environment.

Guidance for applying the 10 principles for integrated disaster risk reduction and climate change adaptation in natural resource management	
3. Recognize rights and responsibilities.	• Advocate to governments and private companies for transparent planning processes affecting key natural resources (such as for mining projects, water extraction and land-use changes^G), and for full consultation with local populations affected by changes to, and exploitation of, natural resources.
4. Strengthen participation of, and action by, the population at risk.	• Provide legal and technical information to populations likely to be affected by projects that use or may have an effect on key natural resources; support them to access information on how such projects may affect their vulnerability and exposure to hazards and effects of climate change. • Provide training and material inputs to at-risk populations to contribute to building a resilient natural environment through protecting, maintaining, restoring and enhancing natural resources (such as mangroves, water pans, fragile soil systems, river banks).
5. Promote systemic engagement and change.	• Advocate for NRM-related policies to incorporate analysis of, and actions to address, disaster and climate change risk, and vice versa; similarly, advocate for NRM authorities to participate in the development of disaster risk reduction/management and climate change policies, and vice versa. • Contribute to strengthening institutional linkages between government departments for NRM, climate change and disaster management by engaging representatives from each in risk-assessment processes, national platforms and forums for sharing good practices. • Advocate for the development and implementation of legislation obliging private sector actors to hold public consultation processes for projects that will affect natural resources, and to put in place accountability mechanisms to affected populations. • Work in partnership with other relevant actors on NRM, including local government, the environment ministry, NGOs and disaster management committees, to share knowledge of multi-faceted issues and to design interventions that meet the needs of all stakeholders. Undertake a power analysis to understand different stakeholder interests with respect to key natural resources, particularly in the case of major development/ infrastructure projects that will exploit or affect them and communities that depend on them.
6. Foster synergy between multiple levels.	• Strengthen/support the establishment of NRM committees at local levels to monitor and analyze local issues and to represent local interests at other levels.

Guidance for applying the 10 principles for integrated disaster risk reduction and climate change adaptation in natural resource management	
6. Foster synergy between multiple levels.	• Support local authorities and communities to manage natural resources that cross administrative boundaries by providing resources for joint planning, monitoring and capacity-building.
7. Draw on and build diverse sources of knowledge.	• Use participatory and culturally sensitive approaches to capture the knowledge of local and indigenous people, particularly older generations, of how natural resources have changed over time and how people have adapted to those changes. • Harness external technical expertise to conduct in-depth studies of particular natural resources, and to present potential resilience-building options. • Foster innovation by providing communities and organizations that have demonstrated effective NRM with access to technical and scientific advice on adaptation, and closely monitor and document the results. • Work in partnership with others. Many NRM issues are multifaceted (e.g. water basin management) and require the involvement of multiple stakeholders and knowledge bases, including local traditional institutions, local government, the environment ministry, disaster management committees, sectoral experts etc., so that interventions are properly designed and implemented.
8. Instill flexibility and responsiveness.	• Identify indicators of sustainability in natural resources and establish monitoring systems to track changes. • Link NRM with early warning systems for impending hazards, and disseminate the information generated to all relevant actors.
9. Address different timescales.	• Include natural resources in contingency plans, both as hazards and as assets at risk. • Support ongoing NRM initiatives as a 'good enough' starting point for building disaster and climate change resilience; identify suitable ways to introduce thinking about adaptation, and provide resources for experimentation/innovation.
10. Do no harm.	• Take steps to ensure that all programs with a potential for causing a negative impact on the environment are properly assessed prior to implementation (through environmental impact assessment) or, if they already exist, that they are screened for any negative environmental impacts. • Consider the environmental impacts of all post-disaster reconstruction. 'Building back better[G]' means ensuring that responses do not negatively impact the environment and natural resources upon which people depend.

CASE STUDY: HUMBO COMMUNITY-BASED NATURAL REGENERATION PROJECT[55]

Ethiopia, World Vision Ethiopia

The mountainous terrain in the Humbo region of Ethiopia is highly degraded, rugged and chronically drought-prone, and soil erosion is a severe problem. Poverty, hunger and a growing demand for agricultural land have driven local communities to over-exploit forest resources, and deforestation threatens groundwater reserves. Climate change is likely to compound Humbo's vulnerability to natural disasters and poverty.[56] With a population that depends heavily on agriculture for their livelihoods, increasing droughts and floods will create poverty traps for many households, thwarting their efforts to build up assets and invest in a better future. Increased rainfall intensity will lead to even further soil erosion, while prolonged dry spells will be experienced.

In 2005, World Vision identified the natural regeneration of the still-living stumps of felled trees as a means to stimulate ongoing community development and to test new funding streams such as the Clean Development Mechanism (CDM). Developed under the Kyoto Protocol, the CDM allows for reforestation projects to earn carbon credits for each tonne of carbon dioxide equivalent sequestered, or absorbed, by the forest.

After two years of consultation with Humbo zonal level-participants (federal, regional, zonal and district level government bodies) and planning, the Humbo Community-based Natural Regeneration Project became Ethiopia's first Land Use, Land Use Change and Forestry (LULUCF) carbon-trading initiative under the CDM. Recognizing the link between forest preservation and the protection of livelihoods, the twin goals of this project are to mitigate climate change and alleviate poverty through reforestation.

The project uses the Farmer Managed Natural Regeneration[G] (FMNR) technique developed by World Vision, and reflects a **'do no harm'** approach by strengthening community resilience, while also restoring and enhancing the natural environment. The project provides a more cost-effective alternative to the conventional approaches to reforestation from nursery stock by using living stumps instead. To supplement the FMNR, more than 450,000 seedlings a year are being raised in nurseries to restore bare patches of the forest where no living stumps remained.

The project involved the regeneration of 2,728 hectares of degraded native forests with indigenous, bio-diverse species, which act as a 'carbon sink' to mitigate climate change and build environmental, social and economic resilience for future climate change impacts. Technical capacity building was strengthened through training in the Farmer Managed Natural Regeneration technique of community ownership and managed forestry, and more complex and sustainable production systems.

Seven village-level cooperatives formed by the community are responsible for the management and protection of the regenerated forest area. World Vision staff are providing technical training and building the capacity[G] of the cooperatives' members. Much effort has also been invested in community consultation, education and awareness building around the concept of carbon trading. World Vision used drawings, diagrams, and sketches to convey the meaning of carbon sequestration. Theater/drama and radio and TV were used to help communities understand carbon sequestration as well as consultations to allow for questions to be answered.

Through *fostering systemic engagement and change*, and a **'do no harm'** approach, this project will contribute to long-term gains that alleviate poverty while addressing climate change through improved NRM. Within a year of the project's inception, the forest was showing rapid re-vegetation. Four years later, 2,728 hectares of degraded forest that were being continually exploited for wood, charcoal and fodder extraction, had been protected and were being restored and sustainably managed. Over the 30-year crediting period, it is estimated that more than 870,000 metric tonnes of carbon dioxide equivalent will be removed from the atmosphere, helping mitigate climate change and providing a source of income for the community cooperatives.

Sustainable community-led management of the restored forests also produces direct tangible benefits for the wellbeing of local communities. (1) Forest restoration has resulted in increased production of wood and tree products, including honey, medicine, fiber, fruit and wildlife that contribute to household economies. (2) Improved land management has stimulated grass growth, providing fodder for livestock, and can be cut and sold as an additional source of income. (3) Reforestation is also reducing land degradation and soil erosion.

Tools and resources

For information and links, see *Tools and resources* p.146.

4.4   Water, sanitation and hygiene (WASH)

Water supply, sanitation and hygiene—known by the acronym WASH—are fundamental to life and health, yet one quarter of the developing world's population still lacks safe drinking water, and almost half still lacks safe sanitation facilities.[57]

Global demand for improved and extended WASH coverage is increasing due to population growth, urbanization and other factors, while environmental degradation and the growth of water-heavy industries and technology is creating greater competition for limited water resources.

In addition to expanding coverage so that every man, woman and child's right to water and sanitation is fulfilled, all WASH services and installations need to be made resilient to hazards and the effects of climate change in order for them and their benefits to be sustainable.

Key issues

People living in areas where WASH services are exposed to hazards experience high levels of risk. For example, earthquakes and landslides can damage wells and piped-water distribution systems; floods and volcanic eruptions can contaminate water sources; and droughts can cause wells to dry up temporarily or permanently, and prevent sewerage networks from functioning adequately. All types of hazards can also impair hygiene practices that are dependent on a predictable supply of water and functioning sanitation services.

Climate change projections indicate that there will be significant changes to the global water cycle, causing unpredictability in water availability and increasing the likelihood of damage and disruption to drinking water and sanitation infrastructure systems that were designed for a specific range of conditions.[58]

Climate-induced water stress is also predicted to cause competition and tension between different types of water users, such as pastoralists, agriculturalists, and water-dependent industries, potentially leading to migration, conflict and displacement (see section *5.1 Conflict settings* for further details and guidance for practitioners in conflict settings).

Resilient WASH systems enable their users to enjoy good health and develop productive, stable livelihoods. Underground water pans can store water for livestock and human consumption during drought periods, and urban drainage canals cleared ahead of a hurricane season can prevent the accumulation of flood water, reducing risks associated with stagnant water and water-borne disease. WASH systems that are designed on the basis of future disaster and climate information are more likely to cope with the impact of extreme events and increased temperatures, thus facilitating other forms of adaptation for their users.

Guidance for applying the 10 principles for integrated disaster risk reduction and climate change adaptation principles in WASH	
1. Increase understanding of the hazard and climate change context.	• Identify the projected effects of climate change on water availability in the program location, as well as at a wider geographical scale. • Analyze the hazard profile of the program location using the best available information on how hydro-meteorological hazards are likely to be affected by climate change.
2. Increase understanding of exposure, vulnerability and capacity.	• Assess the extent to which current WASH systems in the program location are exposed to hazards and the projected impacts of climate change on surface and groundwater sources. • Assess access to water and sanitation services by the target population, its impact on their health and nutritional status, and how it creates vulnerability to hazards and the effects of climate change. • Conduct hygiene-focused Knowledge, Attitudes and Practices[G] (KAP) surveys among at-risk populations to identify causes of vulnerability and capacities for resilience.
3. Recognize rights and responsibilities.	• Share the results of assessments, surveys and other studies with government ministries (water, health, environment, and others) as duty-bearers for WASH, and other relevant stakeholders such as private companies contracted to supply WASH services. • Raise awareness among at-risk populations of their rights to water and sanitation and how these are affected by disaster and climate change risk.
4. Strengthen participation of, and action by, the population at risk.	• Develop the capacity of local health personnel and representatives of at-risk populations to provide information on measures to take before, during and after common hazards. • Support the formation of WASH committees within at-risk populations; train them to monitor and maintain WASH systems and to negotiate with external service providers.
5. Promote systemic engagement and change.	• Advocate for the engagement of WASH actors (governmental, non-governmental and private sector) in national platforms/forums for disaster risk reduction and climate change adaptation.
6. Foster synergy between multiple levels.	• Identify national laws and policies relevant to WASH issues and climate and disaster risk, and support at-risk populations to advocate for their implementation. • Promote coordination between all water users and authorities within river basin catchments and aquifer recharge zones.

Guidance for applying the 10 principles for integrated disaster risk reduction and climate change adaptation principles in WASH	
7. Draw on and build diverse sources of knowledge.	• Before designing interventions, obtain technical assessments of current groundwater and surface water sources, and the potential impact of climate change on them. • Support the use of traditional water and sanitation practices, where still appropriate, such as water harvesting and storage methods in drought-prone areas. • Share examples of hazard- and climate-resilient WASH systems in other locations, to encourage replication, where appropriate.
8. Instill flexibility and responsiveness.	• Design/retrofit WASH systems to be functional in a range of predicted climate scenarios (e.g. drought and flooding). • Promote systematic monitoring of WASH installations following hazards and in different climatic conditions, and undertake/advocate for improvements where necessary.
9. Address different timescales.	• Support users and service providers to identify early warning indicators for hazards that may affect WASH systems, and to develop contingency plans. • Reduce longer-term vulnerability and exposure[G] by combining emergency measures and the development of sustainable, resilient systems in post-disaster WASH interventions.
10. Do no harm.	• Undertake an environmental impact assessment[G] prior to any intervention. • Systematically monitor groundwater quality and potability, to prevent consumption of contaminated water. • Promote communication and coordination between different water user groups whose access to water is likely to be affected by climate change. • Promote the development of WASH systems that are climate and hazard-resilient, _and_ sustainable in terms of the resources and expertise available locally to maintain them.

Box 4.8: Examples of WASH interventions that promote resilience to hazards and adaptation to climate change

- Raised hand-wells and well-head protection in flood-prone areas, to ensure continuity of access to water during flooding.

- Rainwater harvesting and storage systems for populations in areas without piped water, or in those which experience recurrent drought.

- De-silting of water pans for use by livestock during drought.

- Promotion of household water filters and education on their use, to reduce general morbidity from water-borne disease, and to provide an alternative in the event of damage to WASH installations.

- Raised latrines put at a safe distance from water sources, to prevent overflow and contamination during flooding.

- Modified sanitation systems that use less water and are thus less vulnerable in periods of drought.

- Hygiene and hand-washing campaigns among at-risk populations, to reduce general morbidity; scale-up of campaigns prior to predictable hazards or in response to unusual climatic conditions.

- Clean-up campaigns of drainage canals prior to predicted tropical storms and flash floods.

- Installation of water structures away from seasonal rivers.

CASE STUDY: POST-CYCLONE IMPROVED WATER SANITATION AND HYGIENE, AND LIVELIHOODS RECOVERY[59]

India, CARE India/ CARE International

Cyclone Aila hit India's northeastern coast in 2009, affecting almost 6.6 million people across 18 districts and destroying homes, crops, fisheries and livestock. In the Sundarbans area—a unique ecosystem formed by the confluence of three rivers flowing through India and Bangladesh, with mangroves, saltwater swamps, and a rich variety of flora and fauna—local communities live under the constant threat of cyclones and other natural hazards, and the boundaries between land and water are being continuously redefined. The increased burden of a growing human population and the impact of climate change has made the Sundarbans even more fragile.

After working with the community to identify their needs, CARE India implemented the ECHO-funded Sundarban Aila Recovery Project that provided shelter, helped strengthen livelihoods, and improved water, sanitation and hygiene to communities through multiple interventions.

Five months after Aila, many villages were still inundated with salt water, and there was a desperate need for shelter, food, and water, sanitation and hygiene services (WASH). CARE India designed the project based on villagers'-identified needs with forward planning to reduce risks to future disasters. These included cash-for-work activities, provision of saline-resistant seed varieties, tillage support for cultivation of paddy seeds provided, fish seeds, livestock and poultry, horticultural saplings and vegetable seeds for promoting kitchen gardens. Technical support to promote the preparation and use of organic manure and the establishment of grain banks was also provided. The villagers were involved in project planning and implementation, and contributed labor. Project monitoring committees, consisting of village members, were established for each of the project villages, and were responsible for the overall monitoring of interventions.

To address the WASH issues, CARE India installed raised hand pumps to ensure they would continue to be operational during flooding. These were designed so that they were accessible by people with disabilities. Sites for the hand pumps were chosen in consultation with the community and village council representatives. Community water-user committees were established for each well, and made responsible for maintaining records of user contributions and other matters relating to the wells.

In addition, WASH experts from Water for People conducted 28 training/awareness programs for all core committee members where about 2,000 people learned pump maintenance, basic management and administration, and the importance of cleanliness and hygiene in and around the well and in households, and appropriate usage of pond water; a traditional water source for the community.

Sustainability was enhanced by *fostering synergy at multiple levels*, strong program participant engagement, strong coordination with several international NGOs, NGOs and government agencies, a cost-recovery system and a 'build back better' approach that not only provided alternative water points but ensured they were equipped with disaster risk reduction features and accessible to people with disabilities. Integrating disaster risk reduction in WASH actions proved straightforward, with the resilience of systems improved by relatively simple means that villagers could use easily.

Tools and resources

For information and links, see *Tools and resources* p.147.

4.5 Education

Education can take many forms, from formal schooling and technical or vocational training, to mentoring of children and youth by family members and community elders.

A right in itself, education is regarded as the foundation for individual and societal development.[60] Yet, in order for education to be relevant in contexts of disaster risk and climate change, it needs to develop individuals' knowledge and skills for managing risk and adapting to changes in the external environment. As a service, education also needs to be resilient, to provide continuity of benefits, as well as stability and protection[G], in times of crisis.

Key issues

Although education improves the likelihood of someone enjoying increased economic opportunities and quality of life, it does not necessarily safeguard them from the impact of hazards and other adverse conditions. Having the skills to find a job or start a business, but not knowing how to protect family members and productive assets from floods, for example, can result in significant losses, including loss of life.

Educational environments themselves may be at risk from natural hazards and other impacts of climate change. Following an earthquake, for example, education may be interrupted because facilities are damaged or destroyed, or because they are inhabited by people who have lost their homes. If buildings used for schools and training purposes are physically vulnerable, they endanger the lives of the children and adults who study in them.

Disruption of formal education in post-disaster situations and other types of crises can contribute to social instability and jeopardize recovery processes. In the short term, children who cannot attend school are more likely to be exposed to other risks, such as exploitation or abuse; in the longer term, missing out on education perpetuates the cycle of poverty and vulnerability.

To ensure that education services are resilient to hazards and the effects of climate change, and to reduce disaster and climate change risk, education can be harnessed as a tool for change to build at-risk populations' capacity to address risk. Schools are an ideal setting for learning to take place as they serve as a hub for community activity, but other local structures can also serve as venues for education about disaster and climate change risk.

Guidance for applying the 10 principles for integrated disaster risk reduction and climate change adaptation principles in education	
1. Increase understanding of the hazard and climate change context.	• Use information about known hazards, historical disaster impacts and the projected effects of climate change to advocate for the incorporation of disaster risk reduction and climate change adaptation in national curricula.
2. Increase understanding of exposure, vulnerability and capacity.	• Assess the extent to which buildings used for educational purposes are exposed to hazards and the projected effects of climate change. • Support training for educators (school teachers, elders, parents, community leaders, youth workers and others) to equip them to teach risk- and resilience-related concepts. • Provide training for vocational and technical trainers on relevant risk reduction and adaptation measures (e.g. safe construction techniques; disaster- and climate-resilient agriculture, etc.). • Use local media and public events to raise awareness of disaster and climate risk, and good practices for resilience, among adults, youth and children.
3. Recognize rights and responsibilities.	• Facilitate participation of the most vulnerable sectors of at-risk populations in education about disaster and climate resilience through measures such as provision of school meals and schedules that are compatible with learners' other responsibilities. • Support the development of age- and literacy-appropriate materials on disaster risk reduction and climate change adaptation in local languages and with examples that are relevant to learners. • Advocate for safe and disaster-resilient school environments.
4. Strengthen participation of, and action by, the population at risk.	• Build a holistic understanding of formal and non-formal educational processes in the local context, to identify suitable entry points for incorporating disaster risk reduction and climate change adaptation. • Involve students, teachers and administrative staff of schools and other educational institutions in community-level risk assessments. Support the inclusion of students in school and community planning processes. • Support the development of age- and literacy-appropriate materials in a range of media to engage all sectors of at-risk populations.
5 Promote systemic engagement and change.	• Promote the inclusion of education-related issues and education representatives in forums for disaster risk reduction and climate change adaptation, from national platforms to local disaster management committees (DMCs).

Guidance for applying the 10 principles for integrated disaster risk reduction and climate change adaptation principles in education	
6 Foster synergy between multiple levels.	• Support the participation of local teachers and education-providers in the development of national policies and curricula. • Support the development of locally relevant educational materials that apply national curricula and policy.
7 Draw on and build diverse sources of knowledge.	• Train educators to understand the value of, and demonstrate respect for, traditional and scientific knowledge. • Use accessible language and learning aids (pictures, videos, songs, etc.) to explain scientific and technical concepts.
8. Instill flexibility and responsiveness.	• Promote the use of teaching methods and materials on climate change adaptation and disaster risk reduction that encourage innovation. • Provide assistance to schools that wish to serve as emergency/temporary shelters during and after hazard events. • Encourage analysis after hazard events and disasters, and incorporate lessons into local and school-level preparedness plans.
9. Address different timescales.	• Encourage schools and community leaders to analyze all relevant hazards and climate change effects (rapid- and slow-onset events and longer-term changes) before making risk reduction and continuity plans. Where relevant, support schools and other organized learning environments to hold emergency drills for rapid-onset hazards. Advocate for/support revisions of national curricula at primary, secondary and tertiary education levels, to incorporate disaster risk reduction and climate change adaptation. • Advocate for the siting of schools in terms of both short- and long-term risks/safety.
10. Do no harm.	• Assist educators and education sector decision-makers to access the best available local and scientific information about changing disaster and climate risk.

Box 4.9: Examples of disaster risk reduction and climate change adaptation related to formal and non-formal education

- **Disaster risk reduction and climate change adaptation clubs**: In a semi-formal learning environment, these can engage children, adolescents and youth in gaining knowledge about disasters and climate change, which can then be passed on to others. This can include activities such as developing hazard and capacity maps of the school grounds, or organizing all-school simulations, which can be shared and linked with wider community action plans.

- **School-run early warning systems**: In many cases, schools can run community-level early warning systems which alert children, adolescents, youth and adults to potential crises, and can be an excellent way of engaging the youth in disaster risk reduction and climate change adaptation activities.

- **Environmental education**: Schools are an ideal location to inform children and adolescents about environmental management. They also provide a good opportunity to explore the inter-linkages between human activity and potential future risk.

- **Non-formal education in life skills incorporating disaster risk reduction and climate change adaptation practices**: Basic life skills training can be practised with learners of all ages and provide a good opportunity to integrate exercises on risk and how to prepare for disasters and adapt to climate change.

- **Training of trainers / school teachers**: Supporting the development of trainers in schools and the community on disaster risk reduction and climate change adaptation can provide a useful human resource.

CASE STUDY: CHILD-CENTERED DISASTER RISK REDUCTION

Bangladesh, Save the Children

Fourteen-year-old Arif lives with his parents in Pirojpur Sadar, a sub district of Pirojpur, Bangladesh. His father is a day laborer and his mother, who lost one of her legs following Cyclone Sidr in 2007, has been bed-ridden since the cyclone. Arif had to drop out of school to help support his family and now works as a sound system technician and drives a rickshaw.

Since joining Save the Children's child-centered disaster risk reduction project, Arif and his friends at the children's club have learned about hazards and disasters. They have collected information from the community by visiting and consulting adults for a hazard vulnerability capacity assessment (HVCA), then prepared risk and resources mapping and seasonal calendars for disaster, disease, and crops, as well as a social map that was shared with community members.

Before the project, the community felt that children could do nothing significant for emergency preparedness and response but this changed during the community reflection and validation workshop where the children's club participants presented the vulnerability and capacity assessment outcomes. The community then saw that children could play a key role in local risk reduction initiatives. Now the children have requested that the community and the elected community representative fulfill the special needs of the children as presented in the community risk reduction action plan developed after the assessment.

Arif tells of how he and the other children became passionate and how they divided work among them to disseminate messages to their parents, their siblings and community members. Children, as well community members, feel variations due to climate change (such as water level rises during tidal surges, unusual rain) so these messages related to disaster risk reduction and climate change adaptation are especially important.

Arif said: "Now I am confident and can share the findings with my community and they accept and appreciate it and I can tell the vulnerable houses how to reduce potential risks of disasters."

By increasing the children's **understanding of the hazard and climate change context**, they became enthusiastic about participating in disaster risk reduction discussions in the community and the community praised the children and accepted them as active agents within the community. The children became more confident and raised their concerns about issues affecting them.

Engaging children in disaster risk reduction can improve the quality of the program for adults as well as children, and children should be empowered to participate and present their results to the community.

Tools and resources

For information and links, see *Tools and resources* p.147.

4.6 Health

The majority of the world's poor cannot enjoy their right to health. Almost half of the world's population is at risk of malaria; childhood malnutrition is the underlying cause of over one third of all deaths of children under five years of age; and an estimated 34 million people are living with HIV.[61]

The poorest people rely more on their health than other sectors of the population because they need good health to have productive livelihoods. Falling sick and needing to pay for medical attention can lead to further impoverishment, indebtedness and destitution. Children who are frequently ill do not go to school regularly and lose out on the life opportunities that education offers.

Key issues

Disasters[G] pose a severe risk to people's health status and the health services on which they depend.

Rapid-onset hazards[G] such as earthquakes and storms tend to result in injuries caused by falling buildings and debris, and can destroy or paralyze health facilities through damage to buildings and equipment, direct loss of health staff, and interruptions in the supply chain for medicines and materials.

Slow-onset hazards such as droughts and flooding tend to undermine the health of individuals and communities over longer periods by causing an accumulation of stress and disease that in turn make them more vulnerable to other types of infections and health hazards.

Following all types of hazards, secondary disasters can occur when people's health is harmed by overcrowding in temporary shelters, inadequate emergency WASH services, food insecurity[G] and violence.

Climate change[G] is increasing the frequency and/or intensity of climate-related hazards as well as of existing health risks caused by climate-sensitive disease. The incidence of water-borne disease such as bacterial and parasitic infections is likely to increase as a result of more extensive and longer periods of flooding and drought.[62] Vector-borne diseases, such as malaria and dengue fever, are predicted to increase in warmer, wetter conditions, and are likely to affect new areas as global temperatures rise.[63] Morbidity and mortality rates are likely to increase among vulnerable populations where health services are unable to respond to the changing patterns of disease and demand for appropriate healthcare.

However, none of these effects are inevitable if disaster and climate change risks are adequately understood and managed. Health facilities can increase their resilience[G] through hazard-specific retrofitting measures, contingency planning[G], inclusion in early warning systems and disaster preparedness activities. The incidence of water- and vector-borne disease can be reduced through, for example, hygiene promotion and effective environmental health management; and the health of children and the most vulnerable can be improved and protected through, for example, targeted food and nutrition security and WASH programs. Investment in these measures can prevent people's health and health facilities from falling prey to disasters and climate change; instead, they can become critical sources of resilience.

Guidance for applying the 10 principles for integrated disaster risk reduction and climate change adaptation in health	
1. Increase understanding of the hazard and climate change context.	• Assess the likely epidemiological impacts of known hazards and the projected effects of climate change in the program location.
2. Increase understanding of exposure, vulnerability and capacity.	• Assess the extent to which health facilities in the program location are exposed to hazards and the projected effects of climate change. • Assess the relevance of existing health strategies of governmental and other actors for current and future risk scenarios; identify potential strengths, weaknesses and gaps. • Conduct health-focused Knowledge, Attitudes and Practices (KAP) surveys among at-risk populations to identify causes of vulnerability to current and predicted disease, as well as factors of resilience.
3. Recognize rights and responsibilities.	• Share the results of assessments, surveys and other studies with the health ministry and health service providers (governmental, non-governmental and private companies). • Raise awareness among at-risk populations of their right to health and how this is affected by disaster and climate risk. • Complement governmental health services with programs that emphasize disaster and climate-related health messaging and improve health preparedness, such as immunization campaigns, food storage and preparation, etc.
4. Strengthen participation of, and action by, the population at risk.	• Develop the capacity of local health personnel to implement preventative health programs that include information on measures to take before, during and after common hazards. • Support the formation of health committees within at-risk populations; train them to carry out routine epidemiological surveillance to facilitate early detection and action. • Build knowledge and skills at the household level, for measures such as oral rehydration in cases of diarrhea; water purification; and safe food preparation and storage.
5. Promote systemic engagement and change.	• Promote/support coordination on disaster and climate risk issues between health, housing/shelter, WASH, food security and nutrition actors at the local level.

Guidance for applying the 10 principles for integrated disaster risk reduction and climate change adaptation in health	
5. Promote systemic engagement and change.	• Advocate for the engagement of health sector actors (governmental, non-governmental and private sector) in national platforms and forums for disaster risk reduction and climate change adaptation.
6. Foster synergy between multiple levels.	• Identify national laws and policies relevant to health provision and support at-risk populations to advocate for their implementation. • Promote multi-level contingency planning for health emergencies, including re-deployment of health personnel, equipment and financial resources to meet increased needs.
7. Draw on and build diverse sources of knowledge.	• Build evidence of links between changing disease patterns and hazards over extended time periods to inform the development of appropriate disaster risk reduction and climate change adaptation health strategies. • Analyze health surveillance records during and after previous disasters and weather extremes to identify the main causes of morbidity and the most vulnerable groups. • Support at-risk populations to assess the relevance and effectiveness of traditional health practices in relation to climate change and disaster risk; encourage scale-up of successful ones.
8. Instill flexibility and responsiveness.	• Work with other health stakeholders to identify common indicators and 'triggers' for launching risk-reducing measures such as preventative health campaigns. • Include contingency lines in health budgets at all levels, to address uncommon disease outbreaks that may be a result of climate change.
9. Address different timescales.	• Support the establishment of early warning systems for health facilities and conduct regular simulation exercises. • Address weaknesses detected in critical health facilities as a matter of priority. • Conduct first-aid training of community members. • Reduce longer-term vulnerability through sustained immunization and health promotion campaigns focused on eradicating common diseases and those likely to be exacerbated by climate change.
10. Do no harm.	• Promote good health and nutrition as the basis for resilience to all types of hazards, shocks and changes. • Promote communication and coordination between health actors working with at-risk populations. • Advocate for health providers to incorporate disaster and climate-resilience strategies into effective outreach programs where these already exist.

Box 4.10: Examples of disaster risk reduction and climate change adaptation measures in the health sector

- Malaria-prevention strategies that include distributions of bed nets prior to monsoon seasons and during flood events.
- Retrofitting of hospitals in areas of high seismic activity.
- Identification of alternative sources of energy and water in case of interruption.
- Contingency stocks of vital medicines and materials in case of supply chain interruptions/destruction of transport infrastructure.
- Mutual arrangements with alternative health facilities or organizations to supplement health personnel in times of crisis.
- Hygiene and nutrition campaigns using radio and televisions spots and text messaging services.
- Training in epidemiological surveillance for local health personnel and community volunteers.
- Training and equipment of community members to carry out evacuations and give first aid in disaster situations.
- Distribution and training in the use of household water filters.

CASE STUDY: DEVELOPMENT OF CHOLERA OUTBREAK GUIDELINES: PREPAREDNESS, PREVENTION AND CONTROL[64]

Oxfam GB

After a cholera outbreak during the 2010 Haiti earthquake, Oxfam GB examined the experiences from its cholera programs in Ethiopia, Sudan, Somalia, Haiti, Zimbabwe and the Democratic Republic of Congo. Based on these, Oxfam developed its Cholera Outbreak Guidelines: Preparedness, Prevention and Control to better prepare staff to plan for and respond appropriately to a cholera outbreak. Lessons from Oxfam's recent interventions have shown that most responses have adopted a reactive approach to cholera prevention and control. Often, where interventions have not been coordinated or where a multi-sectoral approach has not been used, they have failed to prevent the occurrence or recurrence of outbreaks; resulting in high morbidity and mortality rates.

Oxfam is aware that changing disease patterns are anticipated as a result of climate change and is particularly concerned about the increase in disease outbreaks and, therefore, a need for guidance to prepare for the event of outbreaks such as cholera.

In order to ensure a more proactive approach to cholera responses in countries classified as "cholera-endemic" by the World Health Organization, Oxfam GB programs now must have in place "active" cholera preparedness and implementation plans that guide both technical and management staff in their roles and responsibilities. These plans also set out what needs to be done before the outbreak season in order to avert illness and death in the event of an outbreak.

In Oxfam's experience in Oromia, Ethiopia, despite awareness-raising efforts in two infected zones, there were still cholera-related deaths, and the outbreak spread to neighboring villages.

Discussions with community members in the zones revealed that some of the messages were too "heavy" to take in and put into effect immediately. People also thought that what they were hearing was similar to hygiene messages that they had heard for years. The only new thing was the rate at which cholera was spreading and killing but people did not understand the urgency of the messages. Further discussions with zonal health representatives and participating organizations showed that community education had been based on routine hygiene education when what was urgently needed was community education specifically designed for cholera emergencies, demonstrating the importance of **increasing the understanding of exposure, vulnerability and capacity** so that the community could understand the issues in their own terms.

Another example of reducing transmission is at funerals. In West Papua, for example, people touch the body of the deceased, after which the ceremony includes a feast. People travel long distances to attend burials, which may bring them from an uninfected area to an infected one and they may then carry cholera back to their home villages, spreading the disease quickly over a wide area. Education on preventive measures at funerals is critical (included in the Oxfam guidelines). In West Papua, Oxfam worked with religious leaders to include proper hand washing after corpses were touched as part of the ceremony, thereby **strengthening participation of, and action by, the population at risk**. Because this innovation did not undermine the significance of the ceremonies, the religious authorities were quick to adopt and implement it. They were given training and hygiene kits (soap, water treatment tablets and buckets) to help ensure that people washed their hands.

All cholera control programs are expensive so it is essential to secure immediate funds to procure vital materials such as household water treatment sachets; oral rehydration solution (ORS) and materials for oral rehydration points (ORPs) or corners; printed information, education and communication (IEC) materials; and the distribution of key hygiene messages on radio or similar mass media.

Practitioners should a) prepare for a cholera response in advance of the cholera season and have an action plan in place; b) ensure that the plan is comprehensive and that they have the capacity to respond, train staff identified, and resource projects required; c) ensure that the cholera prevention and treatment messages are tailored to the target population; d) include an education campaign to sensitize all in the affected area.

Tools and resources

For information and links, see *Tools and resources* p.148.

4.7 Protection

In development and humanitarian work, protection involves seeking to achieve both the upholding of human rights, and the protection of civilians' lives, dignity and integrity from the effects of violence, coercion and deprivation in times of conflict or crisis. As protection is an obligation of states as signatories under international humanitarian law, international human rights law and international refugee law, the role of non-governmental actors is usually to raise awareness of rights, support rights-holders to claim them and duty-bearers to meet them, and to provide humanitarian assistance in situations of unmet need.

Key issues

In contexts of disaster risk, threats to people's rights may be considered a result of the state's inability to fulfill its duty to protect them either by limiting their exposure to hazards or by addressing the factors that make them vulnerable. For example:

- If a school is built in an area known to be of high seismic risk without sound seismic engineering principles, the authorities may be considered responsible and held accountable for the exposure of children to a hazard and/or failing to protect their rights to an education and to life.

- If a population's drinking water supply is contaminated during flooding, and authorities do not provide access to an alternative source of safe water, they may be considered responsible for increasing people's vulnerability to water-borne disease and held accountable for failing to protect their citizens' right to basic services.

- If the government grants a permit for logging in an area prone to heavy rainfall and landslides, without undertaking a risk assessment and putting in place risk-reduction measures, in the event of a landslide it may be considered negligent of its duty to protect its citizens' rights.

The effects of climate change may also result in additional threats to people's rights, including life or people's lives. For example:

- As water stress increases in some areas, acts of violence and deliberate deprivation, such as cattle raids, may occur between groups competing for access to limited pasture and water resources.

- As sea-levels rise, people living in exposed coastal areas may be compelled to migrate. At present, there is a lack of legal and social frameworks to protect climate-related migrants and provide for safe relocation, integration and prevention[G] of exploitation.

- Following a hazard occurrence, such as a flood, women and children in temporary shelters may be exposed to abuse and violence.

- If national or local authorities are under pressure to relocate at-risk populations, individuals or groups may feel coerced to accept 'solutions' that do not respect their rights.

- Large-scale mitigation[G] or adaptation projects such as bio-fuel production and large dam projects may lead to forced displacement or relocation of people living in the potential project area. In some circumstances, coercion or violence may be used to achieve these objectives.

People facing threats to their life and dignity usually employ self-protection capacities and strategies to avoid greater harm or violence against themselves or their livelihoods[G]. In the face of collective threats, working together in civil society associations[G] can increase people's capacity to influence duty-bearers to protect and respect their rights. The role of development and humanitarian practitioners is therefore to strengthen autonomous protection capacities as well as providing complementary capacities and resources to protect the rights of at-risk populations.

Guidance for applying the 10 principles for integrated disaster risk reduction and climate change adaptation in protection	
1. Increase understanding of the hazard and climate change context.	• Provide support to at-risk populations and local authorities to map and document relevant hazards and effects of climate change, ensuring that the process and outputs are of sufficient quality to be used for advocacy and legal claims.
2. Increase understanding of exposure, vulnerability and capacity.	• Assess at-risk populations' exposure, vulnerability and capacities in relation to identified hazards and effects of climate change using a method that enables them to better understand the causes. • With specialist support, use a protection assessment to understand the risks faced by women and children living in emergency shelters following a disaster.
3. Recognize rights and responsibilities.	• Raise awareness among at-risk populations of how disaster and climate risk affects their rights. • Provide training to staff and community leaders on relevant legal frameworks (international and national), and how to use them to develop advocacy strategies for disaster risk reduction and climate change adaptation.
4. Strengthen participation of, and action by, the population at risk.	• Use participatory techniques to identify people's self-protection strategies and to decide on the most appropriate and effective modes of protective action for each situation. • Facilitate dialogue between community leaders, local authorities and other stakeholders on issues related to protection from disaster and climate risks.

Guidance for applying the 10 principles for integrated disaster risk reduction and climate change adaptation in protection

5. Promote systemic engagement and change.	• Provide well-documented cases and support the participation of representatives of at-risk populations in key meetings with governmental authorities, organizations with a mandate for protection, such as UNHCR, and those with responsibility for disaster risk reduction and climate change adaptation.
6. Foster synergy between multiple levels.	• Support affected populations to provide accurate information on protection issues related to disaster and climate risk to policy-makers and decision-makers at different levels of government. • Invite government representatives of authorities responsible for protection, disaster risk reduction and climate change adaptation to visit at-risk populations to better understand the issues they face.
7. Draw on and build diverse sources of knowledge.	• Invest in research on protection issues, particularly with respect to climate change, to increase understanding and awareness among all stakeholders.
8. Instill flexibility and responsiveness.	• Facilitate access by at-risk populations and governments to the best available information on the effects of climate change, so that they can plan—and continue to adapt plans—accordingly.
9. Address different timescales.	• Develop parallel strategies that seek to influence authorities to protect the rights of their own citizens under their sovereign duties to protect, while meeting urgent needs for protection through the engagement of humanitarian actors and the provision of humanitarian assistance if needed. • Train humanitarian staff to identify abuse in post-disaster temporary shelters.*
10. Do no harm.	• Involve protection specialists for advisory support or to directly undertake protection assessments and interventions.* • Carry out a protection analysis before taking any action. • Always act with permission of the affected population and, where necessary, seek guarantees of confidentiality prior to any action.

* Consult any relevant organizational policies on this aspect.

CASE STUDY: EUROPEAN COURT OF HUMAN RIGHTS RULES THAT STATE FAILED IN MUDSLIDE DEATHS[65]

Budayeva and others vs Russia (2008)

The Russian town of Tyrnauz (population 25,000) is situated in the mountain district near Mount Elbrus. Documentary evidence dating from 1937 indicates the region is prone to mudslides and, because these occasionally hit the town, authorities built a retention collector in 1965 and a retention dam in 1999 to protect citizens.

On 20 August, 1999, a mud and debris flow hit the dam, seriously damaging it. Between 30 August 1999 and 7 July 2000, the authorities received a number of warnings from a state agency responsible for monitoring weather hazards in high-altitude areas. Reconstruction of the dam appeared unfeasible at that stage. Consequently, the only way to avoid casualties was to establish observation posts to warn civilians of the threat of an impending mudslide but this measure was never implemented. On 18 July, 2000, a flow of mud and debris hit the town and flooded some of the residential quarters. Tyrnauz was then hit by a succession of mudslides until 25 July 2000. Eight people died, including Vladimir Budayeva, whose wife Khalimat Budayeva applied to the European Court of Human Rights under the European Convention on Human Rights, Article 2 (Right to Life). The lives of a number of other residents were threatened.

The Court held that the Russian Federation violated its positive obligation to protect the right to life under Article 2 by failing to (1) establish legislative and administrative frameworks to deter any threat to the right to life; and (2) provide an adequate judicial response following alleged infringements of the right to life. Article 2 of the Convention imposes a positive obligation on the State to safeguard the lives of people within its jurisdiction. It carries substantive and procedural aspects.

The Court held that states must establish legislative and administrative frameworks to deter any threat to the right to life. The scope of this obligation depends on the origin of the threat and the extent to which it can be mitigated. The obligation applies to imminent, clearly identifiable natural hazards. It applies especially to recurring calamities affecting a distinct area developed for human habitation.

Authorities received several warnings in 1999 about the increased risk of mudslides in Tyrnauz. One specifically stated that record casualties would result if recommended measures were overlooked. There was no ambiguity in the scope or timing of the work needed to prevent such losses but, despite these clear warnings, steps were not taken to prevent harm coming to the citizens of Tyrnauz, and no reason was given as to why.

The Court concluded that there was no justification for authorities' failure to implement land-planning and emergency relief policies in Tyrnauz. Moreover, it found a causal link between administrative flaws, which impeded implementation of relief policies and the death of Vladimir Budayeva, as well as the injuries sustained by other applicants. Therefore, the authorities failed to discharge the positive obligation to establish a legislative and administrative framework to deter threats to the right to life as required by the substantive aspect of Article 2.

The Court held that legislative and administrative frameworks must be properly implemented. Authorities administering these frameworks must ascertain the circumstances under which the incident took place and any shortcomings in the operation of the regulatory system; and identify State officials or authorities involved in the chain of events. Where lives are lost, the judicial system must conduct an independent, impartial investigation that ensures appropriate penalties are applied to those who are responsible for failure of these legislative and administrative frameworks.

Within a week of the incident, the prosecutor's office commenced a criminal investigation into the circumstances of Vladimir Budayeva's death. However, it confined the investigation to establishing the immediate cause of death, which was found to be the collapse of the building. It failed to consider safety compliance and the authorities' responsibility. Importantly, those questions were not the subject of any enquiry, whether criminal, administrative or technical. In particular, no action was taken to verify numerous media allegations and victims' complaints concerning inadequate maintenance of the mud-defence infrastructure or the authorities' failure to set up the warning system. Therefore, for failing to investigate shortcomings in the operation of the regulatory system and identify State officials or authorities involved in the chain of events, the Court concluded that there was a violation of the procedural aspect of Article 2.

This case is a useful illustration of the obligations any state must abide by in maintaining the safety and wellbeing of its citizens, and should that obligation fail, the measures that must be exercised in determining how the failure came about.

Enabling communities and authorities to **recognize their rights and responsibilities** is a vital element in any project to reduce disaster and climate risk.

"As was made clear by the Budayeva decision, these obligations [state's obligation to respect, protect and fulfil the human right to life] are particularly important in the context of disasters that are recurrent. Legally speaking, the significance of a recurrent disaster is that it is foreseeable. This means that governments know or should know that there will be threats arising from physical hazards because they have witnessed those threats unfold in the past. Governments are therefore on notice that the threat to life exists and should take appropriate measures to respect, protect and fulfil rights in the context of foreseeable threats." [66]

Tools and resources

For information and links, see *Tools and resources* p.149.

5

KEY CONTEXTS
FOR DISASTER RISK REDUCTION AND CLIMATE CHANGE ADAPTATION

Chapter 5 is designed to help development and humanitarian practitioners apply disaster risk reduction^G and climate change adaptation^G concepts and good practices in four specific programming contexts: conflict^G, early recovery^G, urban, and slow-onset disasters^G. It includes:

- *Explanations* of:
  - Main characteristics of each context and its relevance for disaster risk reduction and climate change adaptation programming.
  - Key issues in relation to disaster and climate change risk and the key sectors of livelihoods^G, food security, natural resource management^G, WASH, education, health, and protection.[67]

- *Guidelines* for applying an integrated approach to disaster risk reduction and climate change adaptation in different contexts, including application of the 10 principles.

- *Case studies* of disaster risk reduction, climate change adaptation and key sectors in each context.

- Links to *Tools and resources* to implement disaster risk reduction and climate change adaptation in key contexts.

5.1 Conflict settings

Characteristics of a conflict setting

For development and humanitarian agencies and practitioners, conflict settings are those in which different sectors of society disagree about how power and/or resources are being used, and take action to prevent each other from pursuing their interests.[68] They can be at any level, from local to national, across national borders, or involve multiple nations and global institutions. They can involve different levels of hostility between the groups 'in conflict', ranging from tense posturing, to physical, psychological and armed violence. Some conflicts develop rapidly, and are resolved rapidly; others are protracted, latent or recurrent. Yet despite the wide spectrum of conflict settings, most share the following characteristics:

- The issues being disputed have their roots in structural inequities related to the distribution of power and resources in a society.
- They tend to occur in situations of poor or fragile governance[G].
- They are volatile, and conflict may worsen if interventions are insensitive to their dynamics.
- They offer opportunities to generate profound structural change.
- They negatively affect the rights of the affected population through deprivation and by constraining development.
- They generate insecurity for the affected population and other stakeholders[G] present.

Disaster risk reduction and climate change adaptation in conflict settings

Conflict settings are not immune to multiple disasters[G]. In fact, conflict[G] often co-exists with disaster risk[69] for the following reasons:

The root causes of conflict—structural inequities in the distribution of power and resources among the population of a country or region—are also causes of vulnerability[G] and exposure[G] to natural hazards[G]. By extension, the conditions of vulnerability that make certain social groups more likely to experience conflict and disaster, such as economic poverty and social marginalization, are also similar.

Violent conflict can exacerbate and perpetuate disaster risk.[70] When people lose their lives, homes and livelihoods[G] in acts of violence, or due to the threat of violence; their physical and economic vulnerability to other hazards increases. Also, the demands that conflict places on a government's resources can reduce its capacity[G] or willingness to engage in other issues, such as reducing risks[G] that may appear less urgent than those related to current violence.

Conversely, hazards can trigger or fuel conflict, particularly over limited natural resources. For example, a drought that reduces the availability of fertile land and water can lead to disagreements about ownership and customary rights, and potentially to acts of aggression to obtain them.

It is likely that climate change risk will coincide with conflict risk. Global climate change[G] is expected to exacerbate some existing conflicts and contribute to new ones, through gradual changes to the natural resource base on which people's livelihoods depend[71] and because of its effects on existing hazards. Climate-related migration is also expected to lead to conflict over land, jobs and other resources in regions and cities that are unprepared for rapid population growth.

Strategies and programs to reduce disaster and climate change risk are therefore highly relevant in conflict settings, but they need to be undertaken in a way that is sensitive to the dynamics of the conflict; if not they may create additional or compound risks for the affected population. A conflict-sensitive approach to disaster risk reduction[G] and climate change adaptation[G] requires a clear understanding of the interaction between the proposed program and the context, so that all actions within that program seek to limit any unintentional but potentially harmful impacts on the conflict.

Although it may not be the main objective, programs to reduce disaster and climate change risk may also contribute to reducing conflict by bringing together key participants and groups to seek consensus on priorities for improving their lives, livelihoods and wellbeing – thereby building capacities for peace.

Guidance for applying the 10 principles for integrated disaster risk reduction and climate change adaptation in conflict settings	
1. Increase understanding of the hazard and climate change context.	• Explicitly identify linkages between conflict and disaster and climate change risk when conducting assessments and designing programs in conflict settings. This will help build a more holistic analysis, and help prevent 'compartmentalized' programming. • Consider how certain resources such as land or water might impact on conflict issues. For example, rivers that cross country boundaries but are used by multiple stakeholders for different purposes.
2. Increase understanding of exposure, vulnerability and capacity.	• Use PCVA[G] methodologies to generate analysis of exposure and vulnerabilities and capacities in relation to conflict and peace, as well as in relation to disaster and climate change risk. Where similar risk factors are identified, encourage at-risk and affected populations to look for win-win measures.
3. Recognize rights and responsibilities.	• Encourage and support stakeholders to analyze the causes, consequences and responsibilities for risk using a rights-based approach. • Advocate for the development and enforcement of legislation on issues that generate conflict and contribute to disaster and climate change risk, such as natural resource use, land ownership, and the allocation of public funds. • Make available material, financial and technical support to governmental institutions that demonstrate political will to build disaster and climate resilience[G]. Stronger governance capacities may also reduce the risk of conflicts.
4. Strengthen participation of, and action by, the population at risk.	• Use disaster and climate change risk discussions as a reason to bring together representatives of different social, economic and indigenous groups. Learning to interpret information and exchange ideas is an important tool for peace building as well as for building disaster and climate resilience. • Consult all stakeholders (including opposing groups) before allocating resources or defining projects, and be transparent about how decisions will be/were made. Security permitting, advocate for other actors to do the same.
5. Promote systemic engagement and change.	• Develop programs that address issues that have a strong influence on conflict, disaster and climate change risk, namely good governance, NRM and livelihood security. • Advocate for donors to support multi-sectoral programs that address risks holistically.

Guidance for applying the 10 principles for integrated disaster risk reduction and climate change adaptation in conflict settings

6. Foster synergy between multiple levels.	• Include institutional-strengthening components in interventions where relevant, to contribute to the development of accountable governance systems. • Encourage representatives of national and regional governance bodies to visit initiatives that are building disaster and climate resilience in conflict settings.
7. Draw on and build diverse sources of knowledge.	• Document learning from programs, to fill gaps in sector-wide understanding of the interface between disaster and climate change risk, and conflict. • Identify and strengthen customary ways of negotiation and conflict resolution that could be effective for decisions on disaster risk reduction and climate change adaptation.
8. Instill flexibility and responsiveness.	• Support the development of early warning signs of conflict, and contingency planning^G, in order to adapt disaster risk reduction and climate change adaptation programming accordingly. • Undertake periodic analysis with at-risk populations and other willing stakeholders of changes in the climate and their impact on conflict dynamics, and identify ways to address emerging problems.
9. Address different timescales.	• Work with at-risk populations to identify preparedness^G measures for known hazards that are unlikely to exacerbate or trigger conflict; where possible, encourage dialogue and agreement between different interest groups on temporary contingency arrangements, such as evacuation and migration routes, shelters, and access to water points. • Collaborate with institutions and organizations engaged in peace-building initiatives, so that they take into account disaster and climate change risk. • In peace-agreement processes and post-conflict settings, advocate for reconstruction and reintegration programs to take into account the long-term viability of land, natural resources and employment opportunities.
10. Do no harm.	• Provide training to staff (of NGOs and local governmental institutions) in conflict-sensitive approaches and *The Do No Harm Handbook: The Framework for Analyzing the Impact of Assistance on Conflict*. See *Tools and resources* p.149. • Analyze the conflict context before and during programming, and monitor any changes that may indicate that programs are contributing to conflict. • Work in partnership with community-based organizations and networks that have experience and have gained trust in the conflict-affected area.

CASE STUDY: COMMUNITIES REDUCE CONFLICT BY MANAGING WATER

Niger, Mercy Corps

Filingué city in the Tillaberi region of Niger has experienced the impacts of climate change over the past 20 years in the form of recurrent drought due to reduced rainfall and higher temperatures. Typically, during the rainy season, rains fall heavily for one or two hours each day but the ground is so dry that water just runs off, eroding the topsoil, especially where there is no vegetation. In severe rains, the river often overflows and changes the agricultural landscape.

Communities in Filingué rely on rain-catchment systems during the four-month rainy season but, due to recent extended drought periods, water cannot be properly harvested and stored. The drought reduces the ability of animals (goats, cows, sheep) to forage and destroys existing water sources. Many male agriculturalists are forced to move temporarily to the cities to find work while the women and children remain to care for the livestock. Some pastoralists stay in the community but cultivate small plots of agricultural land, while others move further away to find new pastures. Scarce natural resources often bring about conflict between agriculturalists and/or pastoralists over access to water points and scarce grazing lands.

'Pastoral' is a Mercy Corps conflict mitigation[G] and natural resource management[G] (NRM) project in Filingué that set up a local conflict management structure linked to local government representatives. Funded by USAID/OFDA, Pastoral worked at three levels of local government to set up structures in 33 communities linked to two municipalities and in Filingué, to support NRM, reduce conflict risk, and protect the animal assets of 60,000 people who rely on both agriculture[G] and pastoralism for their livelihoods.

The project supported the establishment of a small conflict management team made up of community members from both agriculturalists and pastoralists who were trained to listen to grievances. Creating a community team with agriculturalists and pastoralists and connecting them to their local government helped prevent conflict between competing groups as they were able to establish water-use protocols and gain an understanding of common needs and improved land management. The community engaged in action that preserved their common assets.

The structure also included a committee to regulate and manage the water resource to ensure sustainability and reduce conflict as well as an educational component on climate change and NRM.

Fostering systemic change by engaging all stakeholders at every point of the project and respecting both agriculture and pastoral perspectives, and taking a '**do no harm**' approach to reducing conflict through NRM, were essential to the success of this initiative. A one-year program assessment indicated that the situation was improving.

Tools and resources

For information and links, see *Tools and resources* p.149.

5.2   Early recovery from a humanitarian crisis

Characteristics of the early recovery context

Early recovery[G] is the term used by development and humanitarian practitioners to refer to the process of restoring the assets and services that provide stability to people's lives—home, livelihoods, health, and education—as soon as possible after a disaster. It is initiated in the emergency phase and transitions into longer-term recovery and reconstruction processes.[72]

The concept of 'building back better[G]', although challenging, is generally accepted as critical to early recovery, to increase society's resilience to future hazards and its ability to adapt to other changes, including climate change.

Contexts in which the early recovery process takes place are generally:

- Temporarily dominated by needs for urgent relief, but driven by a concern for restoring self-reliance.
- Governed by national and local authorities and institutions, whose capacity[G] is likely to have been weakened by the direct impacts of the disaster.
- Unstable or potentially unstable in economic, social and political terms.

They may also:

- Have large numbers of international humanitarian organizations and workers present, with varying degrees of knowledge of the area and affected population
- Generate high media interest and international aid.

Disaster risk reduction and climate change adaptation in the early recovery context

Disaster risk reduction and climate change adaptation are key to effective pro-gramming in this context because the affected population's recovery needs to be sustainable in the long term in a hazard-prone environment that may also suffer stresses due to climate change.

The early recovery context presents unique opportunities for disaster risk reduction and climate change adaptation, for the following reasons:

- As a result of the disaster, the deficiencies and weaknesses of the pre-disaster situation are clearly visible.
- There is a political and moral impetus to act, and a fertile environment for extraordinary reforms.
- Additional resources may be available which, if managed wisely, can be directed to addressing underlying risk factors.

- People affected by the disaster tend to be very receptive to interventions that aim to reduce their vulnerability^G to similar hazards.

- The destruction of unsafe infrastructure can create opportunities for the construction of resilient infrastructure.

However, the early recovery context also presents various challenges for disaster risk reduction and climate change adaptation in that all actors are under pressure to meet urgent needs on a massive scale. In some cases, longer-term goals may be considered to be outside the scope of emergency funding. Also, the underlying causes of vulnerability still remain after the disaster has occurred, but need to be addressed in order for recovery to be sustainable.

Guidance for applying the 10 principles for integrated disaster risk reduction and climate change adaptation in early recovery contexts	
1. Increase understanding of the hazard and climate change context.	• Leverage the heightened awareness of risk following the recent disaster to initiate or update mapping of all relevant hazards and effects of climate change (using projections at the lowest available scale). • Raise awareness of the need for recovery and reconstruction programs to be based on a sound assessment of current and future risk.
2. Increase understanding of exposure, vulnerability and capacity.	• Consult local government pre-disaster risk maps, contingency plans and disaster management plans for information that will enable programs to target vulnerable groups and build upon traditional coping mechanisms and local capacities. • Use, and advocate for the use of, post-disaster assessment methods that identify exposure, vulnerabilities and capacities to build resilience in addition to humanitarian needs. • Work with the media to build public awareness of the need for response, recovery and reconstruction strategies to reduce exposure and vulnerabilities and build capacities for resilience.
3. Recognize rights and responsibilities.	• Promote understanding of disaster- and climate-related risk among affected populations, so that they can hold governments and other actors to account during recovery and reconstruction processes, and in future development programs. • Raise awareness among all stakeholders^G of relevant national laws (on disaster management, disaster risk reduction, climate change, climate change adaptation, land tenure and land-use planning, building codes, and others), and advocate for new/revised legislation where necessary.

Guidance for applying the 10 principles for integrated disaster risk reduction and climate change adaptation in early recovery contexts	
4. Strengthen participation of, and action by, the population at risk.	• Advocate for the involvement of local leaders, representatives and community-based organizations in post-disaster assessment processes and decisions about relief and recovery, and support them to identify and communicate the needs of their communities. • Provide information about risk and risk reduction options to the affected population, to enable them to make choices in their recovery process that increase their resilience.
5. Promote systemic engagement and change.	• Advocate for the inclusion of disaster risk reduction and climate change adaptation considerations in Post-Disaster Needs Assessments (PDNA) led by NGOs, the government and the UN. • Advocate for recovery and reconstruction plans to address conditions and causes of vulnerability, including structural issues of land tenure, poverty and exclusion.
6. Foster synergy between multiple levels.	• Raise awareness of disaster risk reduction and climate change adaptation issues in UNDP Early Recovery Cluster and other sectoral clusters. • Share the results of good practice of disaster risk reduction and climate change adaptation within early recovery with other actors, from local to national.
7. Draw on and build diverse sources of knowledge.	• Support research on sectoral models of early recovery that integrate risk reduction and adaptation components.
8. Instill flexibility and responsiveness.	• Promote hazard and climate-resilient choices in construction techniques, materials, and land-use planning. • Build upon increased interest in resilience to future hazards by establishing/ strengthening multi-stakeholder platforms (at all levels) to monitor disaster and climate change risk.
9. Address different timescales.	• Leverage interest in the current crisis to obtain multi-year funding for longer-term disaster and climate resilience-building interventions in addition to short-term relief projects. • Include 'safety net' measures such as unconditional cash grants and community kitchens to reduce the need for disaster-affected people to resort to negative coping mechanisms (such as selling their assets) which would increase their future vulnerability.
10. Do no harm.	• Encourage all actors to analyze proposed interventions in terms of their potential impact on disaster and climate change risk (current and future) and to make the results available to affected and at-risk populations.

Box 5.1: Examples by sector of disaster risk reduction and climate change adaptation in early recovery programs

Shelter

- Provide hazard-resilient materials and designs for transitional shelter.
- Use locally available materials if possible, if they meet construction standards required.
- Train local masons and construction workers in affordable hazard-resilient construction.
- Conduct public demonstrations of hazard-resilient designs using locally available materials.
- Launch a review of national building regulations and codes.
- Launch risk mapping to guide return, reconstruction and relocation processes.
- Conduct an environmental assessment for reconstruction and sourcing of building materials.

Food security

- Use cash-for-work to help affected households meet food deficits while also benefiting the wider community through clean-up and hazard mitigation actions.
- Provide cash grants to prevent affected households from meeting short-term needs (such as food, debt repayments and education costs) by selling livelihoods assets that are important for their future food security.
- Provide improved seed varieties that will help meet food security needs in future climate scenarios. Vouchers and fair programs are highly recommended to provide locally available appropriate seed varieties and allow farmers to select their own seed.

Livelihoods

- Provide cash grants/inputs for restoring viable, resilient livelihoods, and for diversification of livelihoods strategies to spread risk.
- In rural areas, offer incentives for experimentation with climate adaptive and disaster-resilient agricultural practices, such as drought-tolerant seeds, backed up by safety nets to compensate for any losses incurred.
- Facilitate access to micro-finance, micro-savings, and micro-insurance services where appropriate.
- Use cash-for-work for early recovery interventions in other sectors.
- See *4.2 Livelihoods* section, for additional examples.

Governance and institutional strengthening

- Complete and disseminate results of PDNA.
- Support development/enforcement of building codes.
- Undertake rapid risk mapping to inform early decision making in all sectors.
- Launch contingency planning processes.
- Establish early warning systems and training for users.
- Introduce emergency drills for public service providers.
- Advocate for local government budget allocations for disaster risk reduction and climate change adaptation.

Box 5.1: Examples by sector of disaster risk reduction and climate change adaptation in early recovery programs (cont.)

Education

- Provide hazard-resilient materials and designs for temporary schools.
- Introduce emergency drills for students and teachers.
- Teach safe construction for public buildings (schools and hospitals).

  See *4.5 Education* section, for additional examples.

WASH

- Rehabilitate damaged water distribution networks using hazard- and stress-resilient materials and designs.
- Establish and undertake capacity building of local water committees for maintenance and resource management.
- Establish risk-sensitive community-based water systems.
- Distribute household water filters, and offer training in their use.

CASE STUDY: FLOOD EMERGENCY PREPAREDNESS AND RESPONSE IN INTERNALLY DISPLACED PERSONS CAMP[73]

Sudan, Catholic Relief Services

In 2007, flooding caused by heavy rains in Sudan's Khartoum state, destroyed 1,400 shelters in Jebel Aulia internally displaced persons (IDP) camp, where an estimated 100,000 people lived in an unplanned, overcrowded area with poor basic infrastructure. CRS' immediate relief supplies included non-food items, emergency shelter, and rehabilitation of water and sanitation facilities, static and mobile health services.

Soon after relief supplies were distributed by CRS, community members approached CRS for appropriate transitional shelters, particularly important due to Sudan's extreme temperatures— between 43° and 51°C—and the crowded camp conditions. After long discussions with communities and donors, CRS obtained a small budget for the project. CRS worked with the government of Sudan and the affected communities on the design of the project to identify resources available for transitional shelter, including community labor and assets such as available water and soil.

The community agreed to construct their own improved mud block structures while traditional roofing materials were provided by CRS as affected communities could not afford these. To improve drainage in future floods, food-for-work supported community labor to clear water drainage systems. In addition, CRS and the government provided supplies for the rehabilitation of damaged bridges and roads, reconstruction of two of the most damaged schools, and the health facility, and materials to improve flood-resistant shelter for future rainy seasons for at-risk urban communities. These communities were able to repair their homes, open drains leading to the main water canals and protect the most flood-vulnerable homes close to the river by preparing and placing sand bags around the homes. Many people residing in Jebel Aulia have been there for some time. When their homes were damaged by the floods, their livelihoods were interrupted.

Community leaders and members were also trained in flood emergency response including evacuation of the most vulnerable to safer areas, providing key contact people with rapid situation analysis reports on damages and injuries, and mobilizing communities to fill sand bags to prevent further damage to infrastructure and homes.

Even with heavy rains the following year, the camp suffered very minimal damage, and no emergency interventions were required. People managed to retain their assets, livelihoods and access to markets and main service delivery points throughout the rainy season. In Khartoum, hazards may include extreme drought and flood events, dust storms, thunderstorms and heat waves that may pose a serious threat to lives and livelihoods. Future climate change is expected to see these hazards intensify.[74]

Prompted by the community, early recovery quickly followed the relief stage of the initiatives in the Sudan flood response. By **addressing different time scales**, CRS worked with the community to design appropriate flood-resistant transitional shelters and to better prepare for future floods thus reducing the impact on their lives and livelihoods.

The use of participatory data collection and analytical processes with target communities generates awareness of risk and ownership of future actions to reduce it; communities can proactively participate in the design of projects to achieve their desired goals, and can be enabled to identify assets and resources they can contribute, and thus willingly contribute and own the results of the interventions; and disaster and climate change risk interventions can be integrated with those of acute emergency response to reduce the impact of similar future disasters.

Tools and resources

For information and links, see *Tools and resources* p.150.

5.3   Urban contexts

Characteristics of urban contexts

By 2030, over 60 percent of the world's population—almost five billion people—will live and work in urban environments. Such contexts, which range from small towns to megacities, are typically characterized by:

- High population density.
- Concentrations of economic assets and infrastructure.
- A predominantly cash-based economy.
- Heterogeneous, mobile populations.
- Complex governance systems and processes.

Due to the pace and nature of their growth, many urban contexts also have:

- Areas of spontaneous, informal, and (in some cases) illegal settlements, in high-risk, sometimes uninhabitable areas, lacking adequate resources and services.
- Degraded natural environments within and around human settlements.
- Inadequate regulatory systems and lack of compliance with safe construction codes.
- Large sectors of the population employed in informal economies.
- Social tensions and insecurity.

Disaster and climate change risk in urban contexts

For historically strategic reasons, many of the world's major cities are located in areas exposed to major geological and meteorological hazards, for example, on the coast, on floodplains, or in tectonically active areas. In many cases, urban peripheries are exposed to additional sources of low-level hazards as a consequence of inappropriate land use or poor natural resource management.

Climate change is anticipated to amplify some of these meteorological hazards in uncertain ways, as well as creating new risk scenarios. These include exposure to sea-level rise, and intensification of the heat island[G] effect. The impacts of climate change on land-dependent and subsistence-based livelihoods in rural areas may also contribute to rural-to-urban migration.

Features of the urban context generate urban-specific vulnerabilities, such as:

- High-density built areas in locations that are exposed to hazards.

- Poorly constructed buildings often built with inferior materials and with variable levels of building-code enforcement, and the inadequate provision of risk-reducing infrastructure for the size and complexity of the urban system.

- Low ground infiltration rates and the difficulty of making structural alterations to the 'hard' urban frame to reduce or manage sources of environmental risk, for example watershed management.

- Dependency on public utilities, such as piped water and electricity, which may be deficient, be disrupted following a hazard, or be affected by climatic variability and/or water availability.

- Dependency on rural agriculture and imports for food security, which are susceptible to climatic variability as well as local-to-global trade conditions.

- Lack of awareness of local hazards among new arrivals to urban areas.

Urban populations and governance systems also tend to have inherent capacities for reducing disaster and climate change risk, such as:

- Diverse and innovative livelihood strategies that spread risk and adapt to change.

- Availability of human capital (including professionals and skilled laborers) for designing and implementing resilience measures.

- Presence of multiple governmental institutions, urban development legislation, policies, and resources.

- Economies of scale that make protection of large numbers of people and economic activities easier and more cost-effective.

Guidance for applying the 10 principles for integrated disaster risk reduction and climate change adaptation in urban contexts	
1. Increase understanding of the hazard and climate change context.	• Develop and overlap maps of hazards and other effects of climate change on urban areas at different scales (regional, city-wide, and of specific neighborhoods or sectors) to build a comprehensive understanding of the context for any intervention. • Integrate analysis of hazards and effects of climate change with other sources of urban risk, such as technological hazards and social violence. The complexity of the urban environment requires resilience-building strategies that seek to address multiple sources of risk.

Guidance for applying the 10 principles for integrated disaster risk reduction and climate change adaptation in urban contexts	
2. Increase understanding of exposure, vulnerability and capacity.	• Consider the effects of population growth, migration trends and unemployment/ informal employment on exposure, vulnerability and capacities for resilience • Focus on illegal and spontaneous settlements, and on older central districts where vulnerability and exposure are likely to be higher. • Engage professionals (engineers, city planners and social workers) to provide expert analysis where necessary, for example, of construction, land use and social conflict.
3. Recognize rights and responsibilities.	• Identify all relevant authorities with responsibility for aspects of urban development, so that programs may include strategies for institutional strengthening, collaboration, and advocacy. • Raise public awareness of rights and responsibilities for key basic services, such as water supply, sanitation and waste management, which have a major impact on vulnerability in urban environments. • Advocate for the creation/updating and implementation of legislation that strengthens accountability for disaster risk reduction of public and private sector actors. • Support research into issues of land tenure and land-use planning that may contribute to disaster and climate change risk, and promote dissemination of the results.
4. Strengthen participation of, and action by, the population at risk.	• Use participatory risk assessment processes to generate greater social cohesion in heterogeneous urban populations. • Plan activities in accordance with urban livelihood dynamics, which tend to involve greater commuting distances and longer working days than in rural areas. • Provide positive opportunities for leadership among urban youth by involving them in activities such as small-scale hazard mitigation works, training for disaster committees, and public campaigns.
5. Promote systemic engagement and change.	• Identify and engage a wide range of stakeholders (including emergency services, representatives of all relevant government departments, private sector actors and civil society organizations) in city-wide and area-specific forums for urban risk management. • Advocate for and support multi-sectoral contingency planning for hazards events. • Create incentives for, and recognition of, public-private partnerships that build resilience. • Plan for longer and more complex negotiations and coordination processes in urban environments.

Guidance for applying the 10 principles for integrated disaster risk reduction and climate change adaptation in urban contexts	
6. Foster synergy between multiple levels.	• Advocate for the development of national policies and legislation that create an enabling environment for urban resilience-building. • Advocate for and contribute to multi-level contingency planning as a matter of priority. • Support representatives of neighborhood associations and civil society groups to participate in forums on urban planning and development, and to raise issues of risk and resilience.
7. Draw on and build diverse sources of knowledge.	• Encourage municipal governments to learn from other cities committed to reducing disaster and climate change risk, through initiatives such as the UNISDR Making Cities Resilient campaign and the Sustainable Cities movement (See *Tools and resources* p.151). • Support action-research on urban risk reduction and adaptation to meet the growing demand for tools, methods and models of successful practice.
8. Instill flexibility and responsiveness.	• Promote environmentally sustainable, hazard- and climate-resilient choices in construction techniques, materials, and land-use planning. • Advocate for investment in multi-hazard and multi-effect forecasting and early warning systems[G]. • Use the best available information on climate change to develop long-term strategies for environmental health, safe housing and employment generation.
9. Address different timescales.	• Make disaster preparedness a priority, to facilitate good coordination among multiple stakeholders and effective management of large populations in the event of a hazard. • Advocate for critical infrastructure and public facilities (schools and hospitals, in particular) to be made hazard- and climate-resilient. • Plan disaster response and recovery strategies in advance. • Include small- to medium-sized towns in urban risk-reduction strategies, where the fastest population growth is expected.
10. Do no harm.	• Work in partnership with neighborhood associations and civil society networks that have close knowledge of target populations and areas, and are well-placed to identify unintended impacts. • Advocate for post-disaster reconstruction and rehabilitation projects in urban areas to be based on disaster risk reduction and climate change principles.

Box 5.2: Examples by sector of disaster risk reduction and climate change adaptation interventions in urban contexts

Land use and housing

- Advocacy for land-use planning, including provision for areas of low-income housing, that is informed by disaster and climate change risk analysis in addition to meeting criteria on environmental sustainability and human wellbeing.
- Advocacy to formally recognize established informal settlements, as the basis for municipal and private investment in risk reduction and adaptation measures.
- Demonstration projects for climate and risk-appropriate design and materials for housing, and provision of incentives to generate uptake.

Water and sanitation

- Support for diversification of water supply from household to municipal levels, to adapt to variations in water availability.
- Promotion of/advocacy for wastewater recycling at household and city-wide levels, to reduce demand on (seasonally) stressed water sources.
- Promotion of/advocacy for increased capacity of storm water drainage systems.
- Awareness raising and direct actions to preserve ecological buffers (e.g. wooded areas, storm water collection ponds, flood plains) within and around urban areas.

Livelihoods

- Provision of grants/access to credit and training for livelihoods diversification and adapting livelihoods to climate change.
- Promotion of micro-insurance for housing and livelihoods assets.
- Promotion of safe working conditions and continuity of employment/compensation for workers in factories, local industries, etc.
- Development of household or community sites for urban agriculture, such as raised plant beds and shared allotments, for domestic consumption and income-generation. Where possible, use recycled waste water for irrigation.

Disaster preparedness

- Raising awareness of disaster and climate change risk through education and training programs, and community sports or social events.
- Provision of training and/or equipment to local and municipal disaster response personnel.
- Raising awareness among city-level disaster response personnel of their respective responsibilities relative to each other and the national platform, and of protocol for any central coordination of preparation and response, to ensure all activities are complementary.
- Support for/development of community-level early warning and evacuation systems using appropriate media and technology. In some urban areas, social media platforms and cell phones may provide the most effective means for mass communication.
- Promotion of agreements on cooperation between cities for mutual support in times of emergency.

Box 5.2: Examples by sector of disaster risk reduction and climate change adaptation interventions in urban contexts (cont.)

- Recognition that the most effective disaster risk reduction and climate change adaptation activities also meet present day needs and priorities for communities and cities.
- Advocacy/promotion of safe location of warehouses and other emergency facilities.
- Specific incorporation of gender and age differences in risk reduction and response activities.

CASE STUDY: PREVENTION AND MITIGATION OF DISASTER RISK IN A SLUM

Guatemala, Multiple partner organizations – local authorities (several departments), CBOs, LNGOs, INGOs including Oxfam

Hurricane Mitch (1998) resulted in considerable loss and damage in Guatemala, and highlighted the vulnerability of Guatemala City's slums. To increase the resilience of poor urban populations in Guatemala City, a series of multi-agency disaster risk reduction projects in a number of slum communities was launched. The approach was holistic and, while the goal was officially disaster risk reduction, it resulted in the general upgrading of the slums.

The projects were developed in communities exposed mainly to landslides, floods, earthquakes, and epidemics (fecal-oral infections, dengue fever). Some of the main vulnerabilities were limited attention by authorities to slums, negative perception of slums by formal society, relatively poor social cohesion, poverty, high gradients, and inadequate infrastructure. Criminality and the risk of violence were also factors that elevated the risk level of these urban neighborhoods.

The selection of communities to participate in the project was based on a number of strict criteria, and more than 30 communities were assessed, of which four qualified. The project teams worked with the target communities to improve infrastructure such as footpaths that doubled as storm water drainage systems, drainage systems, retention walls, access structures, reforestation, water distribution systems, small-bore sewerage systems and communal halls; capacity building through training and reinforcement of existing community committees and community members and the provision of materials for better community organization; and the strengthening of links to authorities through close collaboration and society, through advocacy.

The project resulted in the construction of more than 5km of footpaths and stairs that serve as drainage channels in the rainy season, more than 3km of retention walls, and 2.5km of small-bore sewerage systems. The cost for rehabilitation construction was about US$60 per community member.

The initiative revealed that: (a) the aims of organizations and of communities are not always the same, but this is no issue if both move in same direction; (b) a multitude of partners are needed to ensure that the skills and the authority needed to act are combined; (c) there is a need to incorporate advocacy if the vulnerability of slums is to be addressed and underlying causes addressed, and (d) quickly solving issues the community is facing, even when these are minor in scale, shows the project is serious and improves the validation and acceptance of the project by the community.

The project focused on the underserved urban slum populations and **recognized their rights to reduced disaster risk and their responsibilities** to contribute to improved structures to better withstand future disasters.

Tools and resources

For information and links, see *Tools and resources* p.151.

5.4 Slow-onset disasters

Characteristics of a slow-onset disaster context

'Slow onset' is the term used by development and humanitarian practitioners to refer to a disaster[G] that does not result from a single, distinct hazard, but one that emerges gradually (over weeks to months and even years), based on a combination of complex and interrelated circumstances.[75]

Widespread food insecurity[G] and famine in the Horn of Africa in 2011 is a recent example of a slow-onset disaster. Drought conditions caused by successive failed rains combined with chronic poverty and malnutrition, high food and fuel prices, unfavorable terms of trade for livestock, as well as sustained and intense violence in some areas, resulted in a disaster that affected over 13 million people.[76] This was despite the fact that there were early warning signs of an impending humanitarian emergency many months in advance.[77]

Slow-onset disasters[G] tend to be:

- **Recurrent** – due to hazards and conditions caused by multi-year phenomena, for example El Niño Southern Oscillation (ENSO).

- **Widespread** – affecting people across large areas, even multiple countries.

- **Detrimental to livelihoods[G] and health** – while they tend to have a lower immediate death toll than rapid-onset disasters, other impacts increase as the situation deteriorates.

- **Difficult to measure in terms of economic losses** – loss of assets can result in years of subsequent lost income and opportunities.

- **Forecasted** – Slow-onset disasters are usually accompanied by early warning signs that can be monitored to allow timely planning and implementation of appropriate responses.

Box 5.3: Examples of slow-onset hazards and conditions

- **Drought** – prolonged periods with less than average rainfall, often causing severe shortages in water.
- **Environmental degradation** – toxic pollution, deforestation, damage to ecosystems, erosion, desertification, etc.
- **Sea-level rise** – causing saline intrusion of coastal agricultural lands and destruction of homes and livelihoods.
- **Ocean acidification** – resulting in loss of coral reef habitats where many fish nurseries are located.
- **Disease outbreaks/epidemics** – causing illness and death of those who come into contact with the disease, for example, cholera or diarrheal outbreaks after flood events.

Disaster risk reduction and climate change adaptation in the slow-onset disaster context

As slow-onset disasters are predictable, providing there is access to reliable information, their consequences may be reduced through early warning and action. In particular, as they are often triggered by recurrent hazards, any action should aim to reduce vulnerability and exposure to similar events in the long term, and build the capacities of at-risk communities to prepare and respond. When a slow-onset hazard results in a humanitarian crisis, it is usually because insufficient capacity or will existed to avoid/prevent it.

Table 5.1: Examples of early warning and early action for flood events		
Timescale	**Example of early warning**	**Example of early action**
Years	• Increasing frequency and intensity of rainfall.	• Regularly update risk maps and contingency plans. • Work with at-risk population to identify and implement actions such as reforestation and reinforcement of houses.
Months	• Forecast of strong above-average rainfall for coming season.	• Update contingency plans. • Inform at-risk populations about enhanced risk and how to reduce it, for example, clearing drains and water channels.
Weeks	• High-ground saturation and forecast of continued rainfall leading to probable flooding.	• Closely monitor rainfall forecasts. • Mobilize local groups responsible for disaster preparedness and response. • Gather resources for short-term risk reduction and response, for example, sandbags, food and water stocks for emergency shelters. • Coordinate with other response agencies.
Days	• Heavy rain and high water levels, likely to result in flooding.	• Move livestock to higher ground; store foodstuffs and valuables in higher places. Inform communities of evacuation procedures, send out early warning to communities.

Table 5.1: Examples of early warning and early action for flood events		
Timescale	Example of early warning	Example of early action
Hours	• Flood water moving down river to affected areas.	• Evacuate.

Source: Adapted from International Federation of the Red Cross and Red Crescent Societies (2008) Early Warning, Early Action. *Geneva, Switzerland: IFRC.*

Climate change is an important factor in many slow-onset disasters, such as drought and flooding, because it is altering rainfall patterns and is predicted to increase their frequency and intensity.[78] It is also causing sea-level and temperature rises that are leading to long-term changes in the natural environment, access to resources, and human and animal health.

Disaster risk reduction and climate change adaptation are highly relevant to programming in slow-onset disaster contexts because they:

- Provide frameworks to support long-term, holistic approaches towards analyzing and managing risk in changing contexts.
- Build people's capacity to prepare for a range of situations that may affect populations/ countries/regions by putting in place hazard mitigation, disaster preparedness and adaptation measures (multi-hazard approaches).
- Encourage people and institutions to prepare for uncertain futures, through scenario planning, and 'no-regrets' adaptation[G] options.
- Prevent the perpetuation or deepening of poverty caused by recurrent hazards and worsening environmental conditions, and break the cycle of costly emergency interventions.

Box 5.4: Examples of disaster risk reduction and climate change adaptation measures to address drought-related food insecurity

- **Protecting food production**: Irrigation, soil and water conservation, water run-off prevention, intercropping, crop diversification, drought-/ flood-/ saline-tolerant seeds.
- **Protecting access to food**: Cash transfers through social safety net programs, food distributions, credit at favorable terms, cash/food-for-work.
- **Preserving food**: Crop and seed stores, community seed and grain banks.
- **Preserving access to water**: Well-drilling and maintenance to improve access to groundwater sources, rainwater harvesting and storage, equitable water distribution.
- **Preserving livestock**: Increasing grain and fodder supplies, selling surplus animals, improving veterinary services and vaccination coverage, access to credit to prevent distress sales of breeding animals, post-drought restocking of depleted herds, relocation of animals to areas where pasture and water resources are greater.

Box 5.4: Examples of disaster risk reduction and climate change adaptation measures to address drought-related food insecurity (cont.)

- **Protecting and diversifying livelihoods**: Insurance, diversification of agricultural production through crop diversification, establishment of kitchen gardens, encouraging the keeping of poultry or setting up of fish ponds; off-farm employment; strengthening access to price information and local markets; maintenance and protection of natural resources such as forests, grazing land and sources of water.

- **Local-to-international early warning systems**: Climate monitoring and forecasting; drought monitoring; household food security monitoring; dissemination of information and guidance; scenario planning.

Guidance for applying the 10 principles for integrated disaster risk reduction and climate change adaptation in slow-onset contexts	
1. Increase understanding of the hazard and climate change context.	• Analyze available data on the impact of climate change on climate-related hazards, identifying new hazard trends in the program location (for example, more frequently occurring droughts, new diseases and disease patterns, and intense rains). • Combine hazard analysis with analysis of other longer-term climate change trends, such as increased air and water temperatures, to build a comprehensive understanding of the program context. • Consider the geographical scale (beyond the immediate program area or target population) of slow-onset hazards and climate change effects and how these might contribute to disaster and climate change risk.
2. Increase understanding of exposure, vulnerability and capacity.	• During a hazard event, overlay population distribution data (and migration routes where relevant) with data about the scale and severity of the current hazard, to estimate exposure; In longer-term planning processes use historical data and climate change projections to estimate potential exposure. • Regularly undertake vulnerability monitoring—using methods such as Coping Strategies Index[G] (CSI) and trends of acute child malnutrition—as a mechanism of early warning for slow-onset disasters and longer-term changes in climatic conditions. • Design assessment methodologies and base-line surveys to include the collection of data about the coping measures (traditional and current) used by affected populations during slow onset hazards, and design programs to strengthen them. • Train and use influential media to understand and communicate the relationship between conditions of vulnerability, exposure and hazards/climate change effects, and to highlight the need for investment in disaster risk reduction and climate change adaptation.

Guidance for applying the 10 principles for integrated disaster risk reduction and climate change adaptation in slow-onset contexts	
3. Recognize rights and responsibilities.	• Use vulnerability assessments to inform advocacy on inequities in healthcare, education, access to markets etc, and their impacts on vulnerability. • In drought contexts, advocate for recognition of customary rights to water and pasture. • Advocate for development of policies and legislation that provide for timely action and resourcing for slow-onset disasters as well as for rapid-onset ones. • Advocate for early response by donors and the international community, based on early warning data.
4. Strengthen participation of, and action by, the population at risk.	• Involve at-risk populations in identifying indicators for early warning systems. Their local knowledge will help to define levels of crisis and triggers for external intervention. • Provide social safety net cash interventions before a hazard event reaches a crisis point, to empower at-risk populations to make choices about the most appropriate measures to take. • Consult communities as early as possible in a slow-onset crisis to design programs built on community priorities (such as the protection of livelihoods), experience, skills and resources. • Assist communities to identify the information gaps that currently prevent them from taking timely action, such as changing market conditions for livestock and crops, and support them to find ways to improve access to information.
5. Promote systemic engagement and change.	• Promote timely and continuous information-sharing among all relevant actors (humanitarian and development-oriented, governmental, non-governmental, private sector and civil society) as the foundation for contingency planning and early action. • Advocate for strong, UN and country-led coordination among all relevant actors to build multi-sectoral early action, and for clear designation of the roles and responsibilities of other key actors.
6. Foster synergy between multiple levels.	• Support and advocate for multi-level early warning systems, contingency plans and contingency budgets that facilitate rapid action from the local level upwards; clarify roles and responsibilities for each level. • Advocate for the participation of local level actors in national post-disaster reviews and policy-making on disaster risk reduction and climate change adaptation; support them to prepare and present information from the local perspective.

Guidance for applying the 10 principles for integrated disaster risk reduction and climate change adaptation in slow-onset contexts

7. Draw on and build diverse sources of knowledge.	• Connect at-risk populations with sources of information about climate change, such as meteorological services, and support the latter to disseminate climate information in user-friendly ways. • Use or generate analyses of long-standing development challenges in the program location to better understand the underlying causes of disaster and climate change risk. • Consult older people in at-risk communities about traditional resilience strategies; encourage discussion among communities and with other stakeholders on the potential effectiveness of these in present and future climate scenarios, • Document and disseminate new lessons learnt about successful practices in slow-onset contexts.
8. Instill flexibility and responsiveness.	• Regularly measure and monitor disaster and climate change risk in natural resources and ecosystems so that management actions can be appropriately adjusted in response to changing conditions, and emerging knowledge about appropriate options for the future can become part of ongoing planning processes.
9. Address different timescales.	• Advocate for the creation of flexible funding sources and mechanisms for early response in slow-onset disasters, to prevent delays in acting upon early warning information. • Invest in preparedness measures (such as grain stores, flood shelters, awareness-raising of the value of timely de-stocking in droughts). • Support or undertake research into the underlying causes of vulnerability as well as of current needs. • Include resilience-building measures (such as improvement/protection of water sources) in humanitarian and early recovery[G] programs to enable affected populations to manage future disaster and climate change risk.
10. Do no harm.	• Take advantage of the longer timeframes of a slow-onset hazard to provide assistance in ways that are supportive of existing institutional structures and social support networks. • Within preparedness processes, consider the potential impacts of interventions on local markets and social dynamics (such as the impact of food distributions on local food prices, and the impact of cash programming on intra- and inter-household support systems) and give preference to the interventions that effectively meet current needs and build longer term resilience.

CASE STUDY: ADAPTATION TO THE IMPACT OF RAPID GLACIER MELT IN BOLIVIA[79]

Bolivia, CARE, (with GEF, World Bank, DIFD, CIDA, UN Habitat)

The retreat of Andean glaciers, which produce 10 percent of the planet's fresh water is resulting in reduced water availability as well as increasing the risk of rapid-onset disasters —such as landslides, mudslides and lake outbursts—for many poor and vulnerable communities living in areas where glacier retreat is most direct. CARE's Adaptation to the Impact of Rapid Glacier Retreat in the Tropical Andes (PRAA) project (July 2008-September 2012) seeks to strengthen the resilience of local ecosystems and economies in relation to the impact caused by rapid glacier retreat in the tropical Andes, in Ecuador, Peru and Bolivia. The objective of the PRAA is to strengthen the resilience of local ecosystems and economies through the implementation of pilot climate change adaptation measures, especially in regard to glacial retreat.

To accomplish this, CARE **draws on and builds diverse sources of knowledge** from the communities themselves local and regional governments and civil society organizations, and by partnering with universities, research institutes and meteorological services.

Communities reported that they noticed an increase in temperature and changes in precipitation patterns in recent years. Farmers have been forced to introduce short-cycle crop varieties that are not always frost- or drought-resistant and rainfall changes affect those that depend on rainfed farming. While most communities noted reductions in glacier size over the years, they did not refer to related changes—such as runoff or impact on water provision—as current or possible future problems, yet such a change in water availability could be a potential source of future conflict. In places where most men do non-agricultural work—such as mining—women take responsibility for agricultural activities and caring for their families making them more vulnerable to negative impacts on crop production. Women expressed the most concern for water quality, and threats to crops and health.

Not directly citing the loss of wetlands, communities report negative impacts on their livelihoods such as: more drought, frost and hail resulting in livestock losses, lower crop yields and changes in planting and harvesting cycles, which were well-managed in the past; increased livestock and crop pests and diseases; loss of crop biodiversity; disappearance of springs and water sources during the dry season, causing conflict among water users; more intense rainfall over shorter periods causing frequent flooding and landslides; and a shorter frost season making it impossible to carry out traditional agricultural activities—such as processing potatoes into chuño (a food preservation process used by families living in the high Andes) —and thus threatening food security.

CARE is using its Climate Vulnerability and Capacity Analysis Handbook to design and implement these pilot projects. Interventions, based on the integrated management of the target water basins, include: Conservation of prairies and forestation to recharge aquifers; drip irrigation; validation of drought- and temperature-resistant crops; páramos (alpine tundra) management plans; validation of soil conservation practices; and development of activities other than agriculture that exert less pressure on water and other natural resources, and are less sensitive to climate change.

Analyses of the pilot interventions highlighted that, in the project areas, the institutional and political framework tends to be either non-existent or just beginning and there is a lack of governance over natural resources. Among the population there was a lack of knowledge about planning processes to respond to the impacts of climate change at different levels, or about policies for disaster risk management. There was also a lack of information about climate scenarios (to back up decisions made by policymakers) and how this would impact water supplies.

Lessons learned included the need to: (a) Adapt CARE's Climate Vulnerability and Capacity Analysis Handbook's tools to the local context so that it provides more information on the specific natural resources a given project will address; (b) Carry out a specific induction for the project team on the expected results of the CVCA and on the four strategies outlined in CARE's Community-based Adaptation (CBA) framework because, while the teams generally managed to generate a solid analysis at the community level, they did not have sufficient understanding and capacity to carry out the same in-depth analysis of the local/ municipal and sub-national levels; (c) Build capacities within the project team to understand and facilitate learning about key climate change and adaptation concepts and the different CVCA tools; (d) Improve the analysis through alliances with specialized institutions and foster better coordination among different stakeholders; (e) Strengthen the comprehensive analysis of results related to climate threats to more accurately interpret what is actually happening at the local level and then design the most appropriate adaptation and response measures, and (f) Schedule workshops at times that are the most suitable for the involved communities to make it possible to collect the perceptions of vulnerable groups.

Tools and resources

For information and links, see *Tools and resources* p.152.

6

CREATING AN ENABLING ENVIRONMENT FOR DISASTER RISK REDUCTION AND CLIMATE CHANGE ADAPTATION

Chapter 6 is designed to help development and humanitarian practitioners understand how to support at-risk communities, and encourage governments and civil society[G] to create an enabling environment for building disaster and climate resilience[G] through advocacy and governance-related work. It includes:

- *Explanations* of:
    - Key terms, basic concepts and approaches relevant to governance, advocacy and the creation of an enabling environment.
    - Key issues in relation to governance, advocacy, disaster risk reduction[G] and climate change adaptation[G].

- *Guidelines* for applying an integrated approach to disaster risk reduction and climate change adaptation within governance and advocacy interventions, including the application of the 10 principles.

- *Case studies* of governance and advocacy related to disaster risk reduction and climate change adaptation.

- Links to *Tools and resources* and relevant organizations for the implementation of disaster risk reduction and climate change adaptation within governance and advocacy interventions.

6.1 Governance

Governance[G] is the exercise of political, economic and administrative authority in the management of a country's affairs at all levels. It comprises formal and informal mechanisms, processes and institutions through which citizens and groups articulate their interests, exercise their legal rights, meet their obligations and mediate their differences. While governance encompasses government, it also includes all relevant groups in society, including private sector and civil society organizations, from household and local levels, to provincial, national and international levels.[80] Good governance for building disaster and climate resilience[G] takes place when capable, accountable, transparent, inclusive and responsive governments work together with civil society, the private sector and at-risk populations to create an enabling environment to improve society's ability to prepare and respond to disasters[G] and their capacity[G] to adapt to changes in the climate.[81,82] It is affected (positively or negatively) by a number of factors including informal governance mechanisms such as power structures, cultural and religious norms and political ideologies, which can also be powerful drivers of risk.[83]

As the governance context determines how people access resources, skills, technology, etc. to protect themselves from hazards[G], recover effectively, and adapt to changes in the longer term, practitioners of disaster risk reduction[G] and climate change adaptation[G] need to understand it. Knowing what roles individuals and organizations play both within and outside the community; how they interact with all sectors of the population and in particular with high-risk groups; and identifying the barriers and constraints to good governance, can help practitioners plan and implement projects and programs that are sustainable in the long term, and that have impact at scale.[84]

Box 6.1: Examples of different types of governance

Organizations

- **Public**: Agricultural extension departments that provide access to information for livelihoods.
- **Private**: Savings and credit organizations that support poor people to access credit to invest in livelihoods or for savings.
- **Civil society**: Community-based cooperatives in urban settings that advocate for the needs of residents.

Policies and processes

- **Policy**: National land-use policies that can help reduce hazard exposure and prevent building in flood-prone areas.
- **Legislation**: Construction rules that set minimum standards for the building of hazard-resilient infrastructure.
- **Institutions**: Power relations in at-risk populations that control access to land, water and other resources.

Source: Adapted from Pasteur, K. (2011) From Vulnerability to Resilience: A framework for analysis and action to build community resilience. *Rugby, UK: Practical Action Publishing.*

Key issues

Disaster and climate change risks pose many difficult challenges for governance. These include:[85]

- **Distributional and equity linkages:** Disasters and the impacts of climate change[G] affect different groups in different ways so there is no workable one-size-fits-all approach. This means that approaches need to take into consideration local contexts, and that responses are designed and implemented accordingly.

- **Societal reach:** Climate change affects all sectors of society. This means that governments, institutions, etc. need to understand a multitude of cross-cutting issues and the interactions between these and climate change. This makes governance difficult and complex.

- **Scientific uncertainty:** Although we know more than ever about climate change, disaster and climate change risk still pose enormous uncertainties, making decision making difficult.

- **Timescales:** The time it takes for positive impacts in disaster and climate change responses to take effect may exceed government tenure which can make disaster risk reduction and climate change adaptation unattractive to decision makers in government.

- **Global implications:** The causes and impact of climate change are international, so the response must be a collective one. Yet coordinating international efforts on such a scale remains a major challenge, leaving issues of global governance largely unanswered.

For disaster risk reduction, existing governance arrangements in many countries continue to fall short of addressing the challenges of those at greatest risk. There is a growing gap between the UN's Hyogo Framework for Action and its implementation at the frontline where disasters impact.[86] Local risk governance has been identified as key to accelerating the effective implementation of risk reduction activities at the local level.[87] This includes: shared decision making between local authorities and local stakeholders[G]; working openly in partnership on technical and functional tasks such as risk assessments, planning and budgeting; and increasing political commitment for local risk governance through greater public accountability. This cannot be done in isolation; local risk governance needs to be supported through coalitions and alliances at national and international levels.

Box 6.2: Example indicators of local risk governance

Inclusion and participation

- Participation by all, especially vulnerable and marginalized groups, in decision making and implementation so that decision making happens at the right level.
- Gender equality, with women and men participating equally in decision making and implementation.
- The specific needs of children and young people are taken into account.
- Partnerships exist between local government, community, private sector, civil society, academia and others to foster knowledge co-generation.

Local capacity

- Risk reduction policies are in place to protect vulnerable people from disasters and climate change (the elderly, ethnic minorities, children and youth, the disabled, migrants) and these policies are regularly reviewed.
- Local risk reduction practices take into account local knowledge, skills and resources.
- There is a local plan of action to turn policies into practice.
- Local government has an adequate budget for risk reduction activities.

Accountability and transparency

- A reference point or baseline has been established from which to measure progress in implementing risk reduction policies.
- Communities and civil society are involved with local government in monitoring risk reduction to make complaints and to get a response when there is a lack of progress.
- Information gathering regularly takes place to collect, review and map disaster risks and climate change.
- Updated and easily understood information about risks and prevention measures is regularly provided to vulnerable people.

Source: Adapted from Global Network for Disaster Reduction (2011) 'If we do not join hands...': Views from the frontline 2011. Global Network for Disaster Reduction

Guidance for applying the 10 principles for integrated disaster risk reduction and climate change adaptation principles in governance

1. Increase understanding of the hazard and climate change context.	• Raise awareness of disaster and climate change risk among at-risk populations so they can advocate for risk reduction measures with government and implementing agencies. • Assess the likely impacts of known hazards and the projected effects of climate change on existing governance structures, especially where these span multiple governance structures (for example, where watersheds span more than one district authority).
2. Increase understanding of exposure, vulnerability and capacity.	• Assess the governance context in relation to existing or proposed programs to identify the most appropriate entry point into decision-making processes affecting at-risk populations. This includes: planning processes, institutions and actors, mandates and decision-making processes, and existing policies and initiatives to better understand how they reduce exposure[G] and vulnerability[G] of at-risk populations and build capacity.
3. Recognize rights and responsibilities.	• Monitor and audit government progress towards set targets (if these exist) and stated objectives for disaster risk reduction and climate change adaptation and report on this to at-risk populations, local government, etc.
4. Strengthen participation of, and action by, the population at risk.	• Increase public accountability by strengthening local-scale democracy (including decentralization of disaster risk reduction and climate change adaptation related activities). • Support decentralized and participatory decision making so that the voices of at-risk populations and the most vulnerable are heard. Power, knowledge and resources are needed at more local levels, so that local governments and other stakeholders can better respond to local needs and expectations.
5. Promote systemic engagement and change.	• Address underlying systemic issues such as power structures, political ideologies, cultural factors, etc. because many of these issues affect at-risk populations and drive their vulnerability to disasters and climate change.
6. Foster synergy between multiple levels.	• Encourage government authorities and institutions to work together to address disaster and climate risk by breaking down institutional barriers or creating groups that collaborate across issues, rather than separate disciplines. • Strengthen links between local, district and national levels through advocacy at different levels, and by establishing processes or structures which facilitate knowledge sharing from the bottom up and top down.

Guidance for applying the 10 principles for integrated disaster risk reduction and climate change adaptation principles in governance	
7. Draw on and build diverse sources of knowledge.	• Advocate for the inclusion of diverse sources of knowledge from a wide variety of stakeholders in governance decision making to support cross-sectoral policy making and integration.
8. Instill flexibility and responsiveness.	• Be responsive to changing political environments and resulting governance structures, so that disaster risk reduction and climate change adaptation initiatives are relevant to changing contexts. • Facilitate access by at-risk populations and governments to the best available information on the effects of climate change so that they can plan—and continue to adapt plans—accordingly.
9. Address different timescales.	• Work with governments at different levels so they can make full use of scientific information that relates to different timescales. • Recognize that issues such as climate change evolve over long periods and may not match with policy-making timeframes, which tend to follow shorter-term electoral cycles, and develop strategies to address this.
10. Do no harm.	• Work with different levels of government to create or enforce laws that reduce greenhouse gas emissions. • Assist policy- and decision-makers to access the best available local and scientific information about changing disaster and climate risk.

CASE STUDY: THE ROLE OF CIVIL SOCIETY IN ESTABLISHING DISASTER MANAGEMENT LAW

Indonesia, ECB Indonesia Consortium, Director of Humanitarian Forum Indonesia (HFI), former secretary general Indonesian Disaster Management Society (MPBI)[88]

Indonesia consists of almost 17,000 islands sprawled across the equator, with a population of 234.2 million people and is one of the world's most susceptible nations to natural disasters, with more than 600,000 people a year suffering from their consequences (2009 UN Global Assessment on Disaster Risk Reduction). In the first quarter of 2011 alone, Indonesia experienced 67 significant earthquakes (5.0 magnitude or higher).[89] Volcanic eruptions, flooding, landslides and tsunamis are continual threats. According to the International Food Policy Research Institute (IFPRI), Indonesia is predicted to experience temperature increases of approximately 0.8°C by 2030 as a result of climate change. Moreover, rainfall patterns are predicted to change, with the rainy season ending earlier and the length of the rainy season overall becoming shorter.[90]

The December 2004 earthquake and tsunami in Aceh, in the north of the island of Sumatra, highlighted the urgent need to improve early warning, pre-disaster preparedness and coordination among stakeholders in delivering humanitarian aid. Interest in establishing a disaster management law became a priority though movement toward creating such a law was slow.

Recognizing the high level of risk throughout the country, and with a view to **fostering systemic engagement and change**, and strengthening the participation of, and action by, the population at risk, the ECB Project Indonesia Consortium initiated discussions within a small group including a range of humanitarian actors interested in advancing the development of a national disaster management law, and a workshop to discuss it was organized in March 2005. Individual stakeholders and 29 organizations participated, including civil society, local and international NGOs, the UN, government ministries, the military and police, resulting in the identification of a coalition tasked with drafting the law. The Indonesian Society for Disaster Management—a non-profit association of disaster management practitioners, scientists, government representatives, international/national organizations and other disaster management entities—acted as facilitator of the group.

A second workshop was then held to collectively draft the initial disaster management law document that was submitted to the House of Representatives for a public hearing, resulting in a response from House members that a draft law had been planned but was yet to be adopted.

Recognizing rights and responsibilities, two simultaneous advocacy processes were set in motion by the group to make the law a top priority on the House of Representatives' legislative agenda. Civil society launched a community awareness campaign and a series of workshops for local stakeholders to increase support for the initiative. The effort to engage multiple voices resulted in the draft disaster law becoming a priority. Within two years, the draft became the third priority on the list of House of Representatives' priority initiatives, up from a rank of 287.

On April 26, 2007, the law of the Republic of Indonesia number 24 of 2007 concerning disaster management was adopted by the government. After its adoption, a National Board for Disaster Management (BNPB) and local disaster management body were established at provincial and district levels, responsible for disaster management (including preparedness, response, rehabilitation and reconstruction phases).

Humanitarian Exchange Magazine reported in June 2009 that: "Progress has been made in disaster management with the passage of the new law, and attitudes to disasters are beginning to shift, from fatalistic acceptance to a proactive management approach. However, it is not certain that the momentum and energy currently evident in Indonesia will be sustained if other threats emerge, for example from a faltering economy, religious extremism or regional instability."[91]

Tools and resources

For information and links, see *Tools and resources* p.152.

6.2   Advocacy

Advocacy is about influencing people, policies, structures and systems to bring about positive change. It is about engaging people to become active citizens who can achieve their goals. Advocacy work need not be left to professionals or experts. The role of an advocate can include facilitating communication between people, negotiating, demonstrating good practice and building alliances with other organizations and networks.

Key issues

For disaster risk reduction and climate change adaptation related advocacy to be effective and build resilience it must work at multiple levels—from household, and local, to district, sub-national, national and international—because issues such as disaster and climate change risk, while manifested at the local level, require interventions at multiple levels, especially globally. For example, in the aftermath of Cyclone Aila in Bangladesh in 2010, the ECB Project country Consortium and other organizations—in partnership with affected populations—advocated at local and provincial levels to rebuild destroyed river embankments. At the national level, this same group advocated to pass the Bangladesh Disaster Management Act. Internationally, the Global Network for Disaster Reduction (GNDR) advocates with the UNISDR to ensure that resources are not concentrated at the national level but are allocated for disaster risk reduction/climate change adaptation work at the local level and that people's rights to participate and inform decision-making processes are upheld.

Box 6.3: Types of advocacy

- **Relationship building (or lobbying):** This is about building relationships with people in authority and starting dialogue to address an issue or a community's needs. It involves increasing their awareness of an issue, seeking to influence them and suggesting potential solutions.

- **Mobilizing the public (or campaigning):** This is about raising awareness through education of the public about a situation—the problem and the potential solution—so that they are encouraged to act. Sometimes, this involves discussing with groups how a situation may affect them, and encouraging them to approach those who have the power to challenge the injustice.

- **Working with the media:** Practitioners can work with local or national media to help convey the message about a situation and its potential solutions. Government officials generally read, watch and listen to the media, so it can be an effective way of highlighting a problem to them. The media also reach a variety of audiences who may be interested in the situation and who might want to get involved.

Source: Shaw, S. (2011) Why advocate on climate change? *Teddington, U.K.: Tearfund*

Advocacy aimed at building disaster and climate resilience is important because both the symptoms and root causes of disasters and climate change must be addressed. Practitioners need to work with those who are affected, and those who make decisions that can have positive and negative impacts on those most at risk. Governments must be held to account; they have a responsibility to uphold their citizens' rights, including their right to be 'safe from harm' (see *Universal Declaration of Human Rights*).[92]

A central purpose and approach of disaster risk reduction/climate change adaptation advocacy is to empower at-risk populations to speak for themselves. Advocacy creates opportunities for people without a voice to speak and be heard and for others to listen; and it helps empower people to become active agents of change (people who not only know their rights, but who have strategies for creating real change in their lives).

Guidance for applying the 10 principles for integrated disaster risk reduction and climate change adaptation principles in advocacy	
1. Increase understanding of the hazard and climate change context.	• Use local information generated through participatory approaches and the best available information on hazard occurrence and the projected effects of climate change, to inform advocacy initiatives.
2. Increase understanding of exposure, vulnerability and capacity.	• Work with at-risk populations and specific high-risk groups to understand the reasons for their exposure and vulnerability to hazards and effects of climate change. • Identify capacities for resilience within the at-risk population, which may be strengthened through advocacy for additional resources and changes to policies, etc. Use this information to inform advocacy initiatives.
3. Recognize rights and responsibilities.	• Raise awareness among at risk populations of how their rights are affected by disasters and climate change, as the basis for advocacy. • Support at-risk populations to hold decision makers and those in power to account through popular campaigning activities. • Support existing international frameworks such as the Hyogo Framework for Action (HFA) and the United Nations Framework Convention on Climate Change (UNFCCC) as they provide important principles for work to address rights and responsibilities in relation to disasters and climate change.
4. Strengthen participation of, and action by, the population at risk.	• Empower at-risk communities through information and education to develop advocacy strategies and action plans so they can conduct their own advocacy and campaigning work. • Use advocacy to help generate political space (participation, transparency and accountability) so representatives of at-risk populations can directly advocate on behalf of their own communities. • Identify, through participatory means, whom to target with advocacy initiatives through mapping of stakeholders, identification of allies and opponents, and selection of key target audiences. • Support at-risk populations to develop advocacy messages that are: targeted to a specific group, focused on a specific problem, action-oriented, simple, clear and concise.

Guidance for applying the 10 principles for integrated disaster risk reduction and climate change adaptation principles in advocacy	
4. Strengthen participation of, and action by, the population at risk.	• Support the participation of at-risk populations in initiatives that lead to the development of a comprehensive and binding post-Kyoto international climate change agreement, which builds on the principles of Kyoto, the HFA, and sustainable development[G]. Support the development of advocacy messages that speak to the issues of at-risk populations. They should be then targeted to a specific group, focused on a specific problem, action-oriented, simple, clear and concise.
5. Foster systemic engagement and change.	• Work with others in alliances or networks to increase the ability to inform and influence those in power, including key decision makers. Develop convincing, objective and rigorous impact evidence to persuade policy- and decision-makers that actions being implemented reduce disaster and climate change risk and can be scaled-up.
6. Foster synergy between multiple levels.	• Encourage governments to integrate disaster risk reduction and climate change adaptation into their national development planning and programming and support government departments to work together rather than in isolation. • Design and implement advocacy initiatives that target different levels and sectors of society.
7. Draw on and build diverse sources of knowledge.	• Tailor the type of evidence and messaging most suitable for influencing the specific target group. For example, testimonies may be more suitable for popular campaigning, and quantitative cost-benefit analyses may be more effective for influencing government.
8. Instill flexibility and responsiveness.	• Facilitate flexibility when designing advocacy initiatives, and be responsive to changing political environments, so that advocacy initiatives are relevant and robust to changing contexts.
9. Address different timescales.	• Support the development and implementation of advocacy plans that provide a road map for short-, medium- and long-term advocacy goals, vital for tracking progress and achieving advocacy milestones.
10. Do no harm.	• Monitor and evaluate advocacy work to analyze strengths and weaknesses, and to avoid advocacy activities that may harm at-risk populations. • Work with local authorities and different levels of government to create or enforce laws that reduce greenhouse gas emissions.

CASE STUDY: RESILIENT POST-FLOOD URBAN PLANNING[93]

Bolivia, Oxfam, FUNDEPCO

Trinidad, the capital of the department of Beni, Bolivia, is a rapidly expanding secondary city in the Amazon region of the country with an estimated population of 100,000. The Municipality of Trinidad is built within a protective ring road that serves as a dyke to protect the city from flood waters. However, spontaneous urban growth has led to shanty towns being built outside the protected area.

In 2007, significant flooding damaged infrastructure, including the ring road, livestock and agriculture[G]. The peri-urban population of Trinidad was seriously impacted, including more than 3,200 families, most of which were forced to seek refuge in improvised shelters. There was more flooding the following year but between the two flood events, the municipality suffered from an unusually intense period of drought.

Following the 2007 and 2008 floods, Oxfam and the Bolivian NGO, FUNDEPCO, in close collaboration with the municipal authorities, implemented several emergency response interventions. Observing that the situation was not sustainable, after the emergency response, with technical and financial support from Oxfam and FUNDEPCO, the municipal authorities created a series of development plans with a climate change adaptation and disaster risk reduction approach. The process took two years and involved the participation of more than 15 specialists including geologists, hydrologist, economists, architects and sociologists. Municipal institutions, civil society and representatives from specific population groups (children, elderly, etc.) were also actively involved through interviews, consultations and focus-group discussions to contribute to the design of the project and the specific interventions that would be included.

As a result of input from multiple stakeholders, a set of land-use and land-occupation plans were developed, with a 15-year timeframe, and a five-year municipal development plan was launched. By 2012, many actions and measures had been implemented including the construction of improved flood management structures, improvement of waste management systems, and information campaigns. The municipality is now considered a role model city for the Make Our Cities Resilient campaign, having reached more than five of The 10 Essentials for Making Cities Resilient (See *Tools and resources* p.151). **Fostering systemic engagement and change and synergy between multiple levels** contributed to the achievements of this project.

Tools and resources

For information and links, see *Tools and resources* p.153.

6.3 Advocacy networks

Global

- Climate Action Network International (CAN-I): A global network of civil society organizations working on climate change to influence policy at international and national levels. www.climatenetwork.org
- Global Campaign for Climate Action (GCCA): An international campaign working on climate change. http://gc-ca.org/
- Global Gender and Climate Alliance (GGCA): An alliance of over 50 UN agencies and civil society organizations working together for global recognition of gender perspectives in climate change policy and practice. www.gender-climate.org
- Global Network of Civil Society Organisations for Disaster Reduction (GNDR): A global network of civil society organizations working together to improve the lives of people affected by disasters. www.globalnetwork-dr.org

Regional

- The GNDR is linked to organizations across the world. www.globalnetwork-dr.org
- CAN-International is made up of CAN organizations working in many regions. Contact details of CAN regions are on the international website. www.climatenetwork.org

National

- There are many national networks advocating on disasters and climate change issues. Ask other NGOs working on disasters and climate change or government representatives.

ANNEXES

Tools and resources

1. Understanding disaster risk reduction and climate change adaptation

E-Learning modules on integrating Climate Change Adaptation in Disaster Risk Reduction – modules 1-5 A self-directed e-learning package on the integration of CCA in DRR. *Raks Thai Foundation, CARE International, Poverty Environment and Climate Change Network (PECCN), CARE Nederland and CARE Australia.* http://www.careclimatechange.org/tools

CARE Community Based Adaptation Projects Toolkit Practical 'how-to' guides on the integration of CCA throughout the project cycle. The toolkit is directed at practitioners, and is available in English, Spanish, French, and Portuguese. *CARE International (2010).* http://www.careclimatechange.org/toolkits

Climate Vulnerability and Capacity Analysis (CVCA) Handbook Encourages communities at risk to analyze the causes of risk and to engage with governmental bodies with a duty to reduce disaster and climate change risk. *CARE International (2009). A.Dazé, K. Ambrose, C. Ehrhart.* http://www.careclimatechange.org/cvca/CARE_CVCAHandbook.pdf

Community Resilience Project Modules A range of project modules that enable field workers and communities to identify risks through critical point analysis and develop resilience, building interventions that focus on the five HFA priorities and livelihood capitals. *World Vision International.* http://www.resilienciacomunitaria.org/

Community Owned Vulnerability and Capacity Assessment tool (COVACA) Instruction Manual Exercises to assist communities to identify likely disaster risks, capacities for dealing with these risks and related preparedness measures. *World Vision International (n.d.).* http://www.wvafrica.org/download/drr/COVACA%20 Instruction%20Manual.pdf

Gerando A holistic, community-based approach toolkit focused on reducing the impact of sudden-onset and chronic disasters in communities by increasing community resilience, adopting pro-active strategies to anticipate problems, strengthening local coping mechanisms and building community capacity. World Vision Mozambique (2011). www.wvafrica.org/index.php?option=com_content&view=articl e&id=622&Itemid=361

DRR Toolkit: Integrating Disaster Risk Reduction and Climate Change Adaptation into Area Development Programming A suite of DRR and CCA tools to help practitioners integrate risk assessment and program design components into long term development programming. *World Vision International (2012).* www.wvasiapacific.org/drr

Participatory Capacity and Vulnerability Assessment (PCVA): A Practitioner's Guide
A tool that uses multi-stakeholder risk analysis and planning processes to help staff and partner organizations engage with communities in contexts where natural disasters are significant drivers of poverty and suffering. *Oxfam GB (2012).* http://www.scribd.com/doc/99334979/Participatory-Capacity-and-Vulnerability-Analysis-A-practitioner-s-guide

Roots 9: Reducing Risk of Disaster in our Communities Participatory Assessment of Disaster Risk (PADR). Methodology to enable communities to assess the factors that contribute to the size and scale of any potential disaster and to develop a locally owned plan to address those factors and reduce the risk of disaster. *Tearfund (2011).* http://tilz.tearfund.org/Publications/ROOTS/Reducing+risk+of+disaster+in+our+communities.htm

Vulnerability and Capacity Assessment Toolbox (VCA) A participatory investigative process designed to assess the risks that people face in their locality, their vulnerability to those risks, and the capacities they possess to cope with a hazard and recover from it when it strikes. *International Federation of Red Cross and Red Crescent Societies (IFRC) (2007).* Link to VCA site: http://www.ifrc.org/Global/Publications/disasters/vca/vca-toolbox-en.pdf Link to VCA toolkit: http://www.ifrc.org/en/what-we-do/disaster-management/preparing-for-disaster/disaster-preparedness-tools1/

From Vulnerability to Resilience: A framework for analysis and action to build community resilience A framework for analysis and action to build community resilience. *Practical Action Publishing (2011). K. Pasteur.* www.practicalaction.org/media/download/9654

Ready or Not: Assessing Institutional Aspects of National Capacity for Climate Change Adaptation A framework of national-level functions that all countries will need to perform if they are to continually adapt effectively, including assessment, prioritization, information management, coordination, and risk reduction. *World Resources Institute. (WRI) (2012). A. Dixit, H. McGray, J. Gonzales, M. Desmond.* http://www.wri.org/publication/ready-or-not

Consultation Document: The ACCRA Local Adaptive Capacity Framework (LAC)
A framework to enable the assessment of factors that facilitate the development of adaptive capacity, including institutions and entitlements; knowledge and information; and decision-making and governance. *Africa Climate Change Resilience Alliance (ACCRA) (n.d.).* http://community.eldis.org/.59d669a7/txFileDownload/f.59d669a7/n.LACFconsult.pdf

National HFA Monitor 2011-2013 An online tool to capture the information on progress in the HFA, generated through the multi stakeholder review process. *United Nations International Strategy for Disaster Reduction (UNISDR).* http://www.preventionweb.net/english/hyogo/hfa-monitoring/hfa-monitor/ *Guidance notes:* http://www.preventionweb.net/english/hyogo/hfa-monitoring/documents/HFA-monitor-user-guidance-final.pdf

Characteristics of a Disaster Resilient Community. A guidance note A document to support practitioners and communities to choose relevant indicators for DRR and CCA, some of which may serve as proxy indicators of reduced risk.
Department for International Development (DFID), British Red Cross, Christian Aid, Plan International, Practical Action, Tearfund, Actionaid (2009). J. Twigg, University College London. http://community.eldis.org/.59e907ee/Characteristics2EDITION.pdf
p. 44 Local participation and accountability in disaster preparedness and response

The Sphere Handbook: Humanitarian Charter and Minimum Standards in Humanitarian Response A guide to anchoring humanitarian response in a rights-based and participatory approach. *The Sphere Project (2011).* http://www.spherehandbook.org/

Accountability for Disaster Risk Reduction: Lessons from the Philippines On the importance of state accountability in meeting DRR commitments with particular case study reference on Philippines. *Climate and Disaster Governance (2010). E. Polack, E. M. Luna, J. Dator Bercilla.* http://community.eldis.org/?233@@.59e9a75e!enclosur e=.59e9a99b&ad=1

Red Cross Red Crescent Climate Guide Step-by-step guidance on how to manage climate change risk and implement adaptation strategies. *IFRC (2002).* http://www.climatecentre.org/site/publications/85

Community-based Risk Screening Tool – Adaptation and Livelihoods (CRiSTAL) A decision support tool for assessing and enhancing project impacts on local adaptive capacity to climate variability and climate change. *International Institute for Sustainable Development (IISD), Stockholm Environmental Institute (SEI), The World Conservation Union (IUCN), Inter Cooperation (2011).* http://www.iisd.org/cristaltool/

CEDRA: Climate Change and Environmental Degradation Risk and Adaptation Assessment Project assessment and decision support tool. *Tearfund (2012). M. Wiggins. Contributions from M. Williams.* http://tilz.tearfund.org/Topics/Environmental+Sustainability/ CEDRA.htm

Risk maps and climate projections A website that combines information about known hazards and the location and sphere of influence of events that have resulted in disasters, with a visual depiction of observed and projected climate change effects. *Pacific Disaster Center.* www.pdc.org *Pacific Disaster Centre.* http://www.pdc.org/atlas/ Interactive Global Hazards Atlas showing disaster risk and climate forecasts.

Important Guidance and Resources for Forecast-Based Decision Making Background information on La Niña, seasonal forecast interpretation, connecting forecasts with appropriate actions, and resources for forecast monitoring and decision-making support. *Red Cross/Red Crescent Climate Centre, IFRC, International Research Institute for Climate and Society (IRI) (n.d.).* http://www.climatecentre.org/downloads/File/IRI/2012/ IMPORTANT_FORECAST_GUIDANCE_AND_RESOURCES-May.pdf

Climate Change Country Profiles Individual country reports that contain maps and diagrams demonstrating the observed and projected climates of that country (not all countries are profiled). *United Nations Development Program (UNDP); School of Geography and the Environment, University of Oxford.* http://country-profiles.geog.ox.ac.uk/

Climate Wizard A web-based program designed to enable technical and non-technical audiences to access leading climate change information. *The Nature Conservancy, University of Washington, University of Southern Mississippi (2009).* http://www.climatewizard.org/

Climate Analysis Indicators Tool (CAIT) Indicators and analysis tools designed to inform policy discussions concerning vulnerability and adaptive capacity. *WRI.* http://cait.wri.org

Integrating CCA into Secure Livelihoods Toolkit 1: Framework and approach A toolkit designed to help practitioners develop an analysis of future climate change that can be integrated into mainstream livelihoods. *Christian Aid (2010).* http://www.adaptationlearning.net/sites/default/files/Adaptation%20toolkit%201.pdf

Integrating CCA into Secure Livelihoods. Toolkit 2: Developing a climate change analysis A toolkit designed to help practitioners understand the degree of change that will occur due to longer-term trends and shorter-term variability of climate through climate science and community knowledge sources. *Christian Aid (2010).* http://www.adaptationlearning.net/sites/default/files/Adaptation%20toolkit%202.pdf

Integrating CCA into Secure Livelihoods. Toolkit 3: Developing a programme strategy and plan of action A toolkit designed to help practitioners integrate CCA into overall livelihood programs. *Christian Aid (2010).* http://seachangecop.org/files/documents/Adaptation_toolkit_3.pdf

2.1 Key groups/ Children

Convention on the Rights of the Child (CRC) A legally binding international instrument that sets out the basic human rights of children everywhere. *United Nations Children's Fund (UNICEF) (2009).* Summary document: http://www.unicef.org/crc/files/Rights_overview.pdf Full document: http://www.coe.int/t/dg3/children/participation/CRC-C-GC-12.pdf

Children's Charter for Disaster Risk Reduction The charter aimed at raising the awareness of the need for a child-centered approach to DRR and for stronger commitment from governments, donors and agencies to take appropriate steps to protect children and utilize their energy and knowledge to engage in DRR and CCA. *Institute of Development Studies (IDS), Plan International, Save the Children, UNICEF, World Vision (2011).* http://www.childreninachangingclimate.org/database/CCC/Publications/children_charter.pdf

Children in a Changing Climate *A coalition of child-focused research, development and humanitarian organizations that share knowledge, coordinate activities and work with children and young people to highlight the importance of child-centered disaster risk reduction and climate change prevention and adaptation.* IDS, *Plan International, Save the Children, UNICEF, World Vision (2007). Children on the Frontline: Children and Young People in Disaster Risk Reduction.* http://www.childreninachangingclimate. org/home.htm http://www.childreninachangingclimate.org/database/plan/Publications/Plan-WorldVision_ChildrenOnTheFrontline_2009.pdf

Our climate, Our future A project in which children are using film to examine the impact of climate change on their communities. *Plan International (2009).* http://www.youtube.com/user/planinternationaltv#p/u/6/ZlzloNdLEDc

Child-led disaster risk reduction: a practical guide A guide that demonstrates the varied, productive and leading roles children can play in DRR. It is aimed at practitioners working with children to provide them with examples and ideas to help them enable children to lead the process of disaster risk reduction. *Save the Children (Sweden) (2007). L. Benson, J. Bugge.* http://www.eldis.org/go/topics/resource-guides/aid/key-issues/disaster-risk-reduction/education-and-drr&id=38480&type=Document

Child-Centred DRR Toolkit A toolkit aimed at child-centered DRR: 1) training children through hazard, vulnerability and capacity assessment; 2) planning, monitoring and evaluating child-centered programs; 3) action plans with children; and 4) advocacy with children. *Plan International (2010).* http://www.childreninachangingclimate.org/database/ plan/Publications/Child-Centred_DRR_Toolkit.pdf

2.2 Key groups/ Women, men, gender

Training Manual on Gender and Climate Change A practical tool designed to increase the capacity of policy and decision makers to develop gender-responsive climate change policies and strategies. *IUCN, UNDP, UNEP, GGCA, Women's Environment and Development Organization (WEDO) (2009). L. Aguilar.* https://cmsdata.iucn.org/downloads/ eng_version_web_final_1.pdf

Gender, Climate Change and Community-Based Adaptation: A guidebook for designing and implementing gender-sensitive community-based adaptation programmes and projects Guidance on integrating gender into CBA programming. *UNDP (2010). K. Vincent, L. Wanjiru, A.Aubry, A. Mershon, C. Nyandiga, T. Cull, and K. Banda. Dr. L. W. Garmer (ed).* http://www.adaptationlearning.net/guidance-tools/gender-climate-change-and-community-based-adaptation

Making Disaster Risk Reduction Gender-Sensitive: Policy and Practical Guidelines
Policy and practical guidelines for national and local governments to further implement the HFA. *IUCN, UNDP, United Nations International Strategy For Disaster Reduction (UNISDR) (2009).* http://www.preventionweb.net/english/professional/publications/v.php?id=9922

Adaptation, gender and women's empowerment. CARE International Climate Change Brief
Brief on gender and climate change adaptation including points on incorporating gender-transformative adaptation in strategies. *CARE International (2010).*
http://www.careclimatechange.org/files/adaptation/CARE_Gender_Brief_Oct2010.pdf

Gender, Disaster Risk Reduction and Climate Change Adaptation: A Learning Companion
Practitioner's guide on gender, DRR and CCA in programming. *Oxfam GB (2010).*
http://www.gdnonline.org/resources/OxfamGender&ARR.pdf

Gender and Disaster Risk Reduction: A Training Pack Training pack on gender and DRR. *Oxfam Great Britain (2011). M.C. Ciampi, F. Gell, L. Lasap, E. Turvill.* http://reliefweb.int/sites/reliefweb.int/files/resources/Full_report_116.pdf

2.3 Key groups/ High-risk groups

Mainstreaming Disability into Disaster Risk Reduction: A Training Manual A training manual designed to improve actors' capacities to mainstream disability in DRR. *Handicap International, European Commission (2009). I. Ulmasova, N. Silcock, B. Schranz.* http://www.handicap-international.fr/fileadmin/documents/publications/DisasterRiskReduc.pdf

Homestead Gardening: A Manual for Program Managers, Implementers, and Practitioners
This manual is intended for use by food security, nutrition, and livelihood programmers and practitioners for improved household food production and income generation. It is a compilation of techniques and lessons learned from homestead gardening programs successfully implemented through the Consortium for Southern Africa Food Emergency (C-SAFE) in Lesotho. *CRS (2008). Adam Weimer.*
http://www.crsprogramquality.org/publications/2011/1/14/homestead-gardening.html

The International Classification of Functioning, Disability and Health *This model is not specific to DRR and CCA, but helps to analyze potential consequences of limitations to a person's activity range, and the obstacles to participation in DRR and CCA. WHO (2004).* http://www.who.int/classifications/icf/en/

3. Program cycle management/ Knowledge generation and management

National HFA Monitor 2011-2013 An online tool to capture the information on progress in the HFA, generated through the multi-stakeholder review process. *UNISDR.* http://www.preventionweb.net/english/hyogo/hfa-monitoring/hfa-monitor/

Participatory Monitoring, Evaluation, Reflection and Learning for Community-based Adaptation (PMERL): A Manual for Local Practitioners A manual that can be used for and by vulnerable communities, supported by planners, practitioners and policymakers across the field, to inform their climate adaptation planning and implementation. *CARE (2012). J. Ayers, S. Anderson, S. Pradhan, T. Rossing.* www.careclimatechange.org/files/adaptation/CARE_PMERL_Manual_2012.pdf

Project/programme Monitoring and Evaluation Guide A guide aimed at promoting a common understanding and reliable practice of monitoring and evaluation for projects/ programs. *IFRC (2011).* http://www.ifrc.org/Global/Publications/monitoring/IFRC-ME-Guide-8-2011.pdf

Monitoring and Evaluation Guidelines An online toolkit comprising 14 modules providing step-by-step advice on M and E design, implementation and evaluation. *World Food Programme (n.d.).* http://www.wfp.org/content/monitoring-and-evalutation-guidelines

Characteristics of a Disaster Resilient Community. A guidance note
Guidance to help practitioners and communities choose relevant indicators for DRR and CCA, some of which may serve as proxy indicators of reduced risk. *DFID, British Red Cross, Christian Aid, Plan, Practical Action, Tearfund, Actionaid (2009). J. Twigg, University College London.* http://www.abuhc.org/Publications/CDRC%20v2%20final.pdf

3.2 Program cycle management/ Analysis

CARE International Climate Change Brief: Adaptation, gender and women's empowerment A document describing the link between gender and vulnerability and how this shows itself in practice. *CARE International.* http://www.careclimatechange.org/files/adaptation/CARE_Gender_Brief_Oct2010.pdf

E-Learning modules on integrating Climate Change Adaptation in Disaster Risk Reduction A self-directed e-learning package on the integration of Climate Change Adaptation in Disaster Risk Reduction. *Raks Thai Foundation, CARE International, PECCN, CARE Nederland and CARE Australia.* http://www.careclimatechange.org/tools

Climate Vulnerability and Capacity Analysis (CVCA) Handbook A tool to encourage communities at risk to analyze the causes of risk and to engage with governmental bodies with a duty to reduce climate and disaster risk. *CARE International (2009). A. Dazé, K. Ambrose, C. Ehrhart.* http://www.careclimatechange.org/cvca/CARE_CVCAHandbook.pdf

Vulnerability matrix Group activity instructions to determine the hazards, vulnerability and capacity related to livelihoods. *CARE International (2009). A. Dazé, K. Ambrose, C. Ehrhart.* http://www.careclimatechange.org/cvca/CARE_CVCAHandbook.pdf p. 39 of CVCA.

Community Based Disaster Preparedness: A How-To Guide A comprehensive guide based on CRS and partners' experience in community based disaster preparedness including establishing community groups and task forces to prepare for and respond to emergencies. *Catholic Relief Services (CRS), European Commission Humanitarian Aid (2009). Cassie Dummett.* http://www.crsprogramquality.org/publications/2009/11/20/community-based-disaster-preparedness-a-how-to-guide.html

Community-based Risk Screening Tool – Adaptation and Livelihoods (CRiSTAL) Information and resources related to the screening tool. *IISD, SEI, Inter Cooperation (2011).* http://www.iisd.org/cristaltool/

Adaptation Toolkit: Integrating Adaptation to Climate Change into Secure Livelihoods. Toolkit 2: Developing a climate change analysis The toolkit is designed to support the integration of climate change and disasters into livelihoods work. *Christian Aid (2010).* http://unfccc.int/files/adaptation/application/pdf/christianaid_ap_update_sep_09_toolkit_7_sp.pdf

Participatory Capacity and Vulnerability Assessment (PCVA): A Practitioner's Guide A tool that uses multi-stakeholder risk analysis and planning processes to help staff and partner organizations engage with communities in contexts where natural disasters are significant drivers of poverty and suffering. *Oxfam GB (2012).* http://www.scribd.com/doc/99334979/Participatory-Capacity-and-Vulnerability-Analysis-A-practitioner-s-guide

Roots 9: Reducing Risk of Disaster in our Communities A tool to enable communities to assess the factors that contribute to the size and scale of any potential disaster and to develop a locally owned plan to address those factors and reduce the risk of disaster. *Tearfund (2011). P. Venton, B. Hansford. R. Blackman (ed).* http://tilz.tearfund.org/Publications/ROOTS/Reducing+risk+of+disaster+in+our+communities.htm

Climate Analysis Indicators Tool Indicators and analysis tools designed to inform policy discussions concerning vulnerability and adaptive capacity. *WRI.* http://cait.wri.org

CEDRA: Climate Change and Environmental Degradation Risk and Adaptation Assessment Project assessment and decision support tool. *Tearfund (2012). M. Wiggins. Contributions from M. Williams.* http://tilz.tearfund.org/Topics/Environmental+Sustainability/CEDRA.htm

The National Adaptive Capacity Framework (NAC) A framework of national-level functions that all countries will need to perform if they are to be adapting effectively, including assessment, prioritization, information management, coordination, and risk reduction. *WRI (2009).* http://www.wri.org/project/vulnerability-and-adaptation/nac-framework

Climate Change Country Profiles Individual country reports that contain maps and diagrams demonstrating the observed and projected climates of that country (not all countries are profiled). *UNDP; School of Geography and the Environment, University of Oxford.* http://country-profiles.geog.ox.ac.uk/

Climate Wizard A web-based program designed to enable technical and non-technical audiences alike to access leading climate change information. *The Nature Conservancy.* http://www.climatewizard.org/

Pressure and Release Model A model to predict when a disaster may occur through the meeting of hazards and vulnerability. *Routledge (1994). B. Wisner, P. Blaikie, T. Cannon, I. Davis.* http://practicalaction.org/media/view/9654 See p. 96

Non-Annex-I national communications and NAPAs received by the secretariat National Communication of each country outlining their circumstances in relation to climate change. United Nations International Conference on Climate Change (UNFCCC) National Adaptation Programmes of Action (NAPAs) for Least Developed countries. *National Communications:* http://unfccc.int/national_reports/non-annex_i_natcom/items/2979. php *NAPAs:* http://unfccc.int/national_reports/items/1408.php

Project Design Handbook A conceptual framework for program and project planning. *CARE International (2002). R. Caldwell.* http://www.ewb-international.org/pdf/CARE%20 Project%20Design%20Handbook.pdf

3.3 Program cycle management/ Design

Disaster Risk Reduction in the Project Cycle Management: A tool for programme officers and project managers A shelter-focused guide for integrating risk management into the project cycle. *Swiss Agency for Development and Cooperation (SDC) (2007). SDC Prevention and Preparedness Team, M. Zimmermann (NDR Consulting).* http://www.constructiongroup.ch/system/files/disaster+risk+reduction+in+the+project+cycle+man agement.pdf

Framework of Milestones and Indicators for Community-Based Adaptation (CBA) A framework designed to identify potential milestones and indicators for projects integrating CCA. *CARE International (2010).* http://www.careclimatechange.org/files/toolkit/ CBA_Framework.pdf

Toolkit for Integrating Climate Change Adaptation into Projects A toolkit designed to guide the integration of CCA into projects. *CARE International, IISD (2010).* http://www.careclimatechange.org/tk/integration/en/open_toolkit.html

Climate Smart Disaster Risk Management: Strengthening Climate Resilience
A framework to guide strategic planning, program development and policy making, and to assess the efficacy of existing DRM policies, projects and programs in the context of climate change. *Strengthening Climate Resilience (SCR), IDS (2010). T. Mitchell, M. Ibrahim, K. Harris, M. Hedger, E. Polack, A. Ahmed, N. Hall, K. Hawrylyshyn, K. Nightingale, M. Onyango, M. Adow, S. Sajjad Mohammed.* http://community.eldis. org/.59e0d267/SCR%20DRM.pdf

Guidelines: National Platforms for Disaster Risk Reduction Guidelines on how to develop a multi stakeholder national platform for DRR to help in the mainstreaming of DRR into development policies, planning and programs at the national level. *UNISDR (2007).* http://www.unisdr.org/we/inform/publications/601

Making Adaptation Count: Concepts and Options for Monitoring and Evaluation of Climate Change Adaptation A practical framework for developing monitoring and evaluation systems that can track the success and failure of CCA initiatives in the development context. *WRI, Federal Ministry for Economic Cooperation and Development (BMZ), Deutsche Gesellschaft für Internationale Zusammenarbeit (GIZ) (2011) M. Spearman, H. McGray.* http://www.wri.org/publication/making-adaptation-count

3.4 Program cycle management/ Implementation

The Basics of Project Implementation: A guide for project managers A guide focusing on the project implementation phase for field-based managers. *CARE International (2007). B.Durr, E. Johnson, J. Rugh, K. Furany, M. Chen, M. Rubio, R. Siles. N. Hussein (managing ed.).* http://www.careclimatechange.org/files/toolkit/CARE_Project_Implementation.pdf

Toolkit for Integrating Climate Change Adaptation into Projects A toolkit designed to guide the integration of CCA into projects. *CARE International, IISD (2010).* http://www.careclimatechange.org/tk/integration/en/open_toolkit.html

Capacity self-assessment A tool for gaining an overall impression of an organization, giving a picture of the stage of its development and providing insight into its current and potential impact. *Tearfund (2003).* http://tilz.tearfund.org/Publications/ROOTS/ Capacity+self-assessment.htm

Ready or Not: Assessing Institutional Aspects of National Capacity for Climate Change Adaptation A framework of national-level functions that all countries need to perform if they are to adapt effectively to climate change. *WRI (2012). A. Dixit, H. McGray, J. Gonzales, M. Desmond.* http://www.wri.org/project/vulnerability-and-adaptation/nac-framework

4.1 Key sectors/ Food security

Practitioners' Guide to the Household Economy Approach (HEA) A livelihoods-based framework designed to provide a clear and accurate representation of the internal workings of household economies. *Regional Hunger and Vulnerability Programme (RHVP), The Food Economy Group (FEG), Save the Children (n.d.). T. Boudreau, M. Lawrence, P. Holzmann, M. O'Donnell, L. Adams, J. Holt, L. Hammond, A. Duffield.* http://www.feg-consulting.com/resource/practitioners-guide-to-hea

Integrated Food Security Classification Tool (IPC) A standardized tool that provides a 'common currency' for classifying food security. *Food and Agriculture Organization (FAO), WFP, Oxfam, Save the Children, Famine Early Warning Systems Network (FEWSNET), CARE International, Joint Research Centre European Commission (n.d.).* http://www.ipcinfo.org/

Household Livelihood Security Analysis (HLSA) Toolkit for practitioners that describes the HLSA and how to implement it. *CARE International (2002).* http://pqdl.care.org/Practice/HLS%20Assessment%20-%20A%20Toolkit%20for%20Practitioners.pdf

Market Information and Food Insecurity Response Analysis The MIFIRA framework provides a logically sequenced set of questions, and corresponding analytical tools to help operational agencies anticipate the likely impact of alternative (food- or cash-based) responses and thereby identify the response that best fits a given food insecurity context. *Barrett, C.B.; Bell, R.; Lentz, E.C.; and Maxwell, D.G. (2009).* http://dyson.cornell.edu/faculty_sites/cbb2/MIFIRA/

Consultation Document: The ACCRA Local Adaptive Capacity Framework (LAC) A framework to enable the assessment of factors that facilitate the development of adaptive capacity, including institutions and entitlements; knowledge and information; and decision-making and governance. *ACCRA (n.d.).* http://community.eldis.org/.59d669a7/txFileDownload/f.59d669a7/n.LACFconsult.pdf

Modeling System for the Agricultural Impacts of Climate Change (MOSAICC) An integrated toolbox to assess the impacts of climate change on agriculture, which can be used to produce different climate scenarios and for economic impact analysis. *European Union, FAO (2010).* http://www.foodsec.org/web/tools/climate-change/climate-change-impact-assessment-tool/en/

Climate Vulnerability and Capacity Analysis (CVCA) Handbook A framework that integrates CCA into development through: climate-resilient livelihoods; DRR; capacity development; and advocacy and social mobilization. *CARE International (2009). A. Dazé, K. Ambrose, C. Ehrhart.* http://www.careclimatechange.org/publications/adaptation

How to conduct a food security assessment: A step-by-step guide for National Societies in Africa A guide for food security assessments for those with no background knowledge. *IFRC (2006).* http://www.ifrc.org/Global/global-fsa-guidelines-en.pdf

Adaptation toolkit: Integrating Adaptation to Climate Change into Secure Livelihoods
A tool kit focused on developing an analysis of future climate change that can be integrated into mainstream livelihoods. *Christian Aid (2010).*
http://www.adaptationlearning.net/sites/default/files/Adaptation%20toolkit%201.pdf

"Climate-Smart" Agriculture: Policies, Practices and Financing for Food Security, Adaptation and Mitigation An approach that examines some of the key technical, institutional, policy and financial responses required to achieve climate smart agriculture. *FAO (2010).* http://www.fao.org/docrep/013/i1881e/i1881e00.pdf

Disaster Risk Reduction in Livelihoods and Food Security Programming: A Learning Companion. Oxfam Disaster Risk Reduction and Climate Change Adaptation Resources
A guide on how to integrate DRR into livelihood planning including case studies and context examples. *Oxfam GB (n.d.).* http://community.eldis.org/?233@@.59cdc973/7!enclosure=.59cf3b6a&ad=1

Mitigating Climate Change Through Food and Land Use Strategies for reducing and collecting greenhouse gas emissions. Outlining five major strategies for reducing and sequestering terrestrial greenhouse gas emissions and six principles for action for the adoption of land-use mitigation. *ECO Agriculture, World Watch Institute (2009).* http://www.worldwatch.org/node/6126

From Vulnerability to Resilience: A framework for analysis and action to build community resilience A framework for analysis and action aimed at reducing vulnerability and strengthening the resilience of individuals, households, and communities. *Practical Action Publishing (2011). K. Pasteur.* http://practicalaction.org/media/view/9654

4.2 Key sectors/ Livelihoods

Community-based Risk Screening Tool – Adaptation and Livelihoods (CRiSTAL)
A framework and computer-based screening tool aimed at helping project managers and planners understand the links between livelihoods and CCA, and to provide planning tools. *IISD, SEI, Inter Cooperation (2011).* http://www.cristaltool.org/

Village Savings and Loans Associations (VS and LA) Programme Guide A guide to village savings and loan associations; their purpose and how they work within communities. *VSL Associates (2007). H.Allen, M. Staehle, C. Waterfield.* http://edu.care.org/Documents/VSLA%20Program%20Guide_Field%20Operations%20Manual%20v.%202.9.pdf

Livelihoods Connect Website containing tools and resources related to the Sustainable Livelihoods Approach (SLA). *Eldis.* http://www.eldis.org/go/livelihoods/

Adapting to Climate Variability and Change: A Guidance Manual for Development Planning A manual for integrating climate change into development projects. *United States Agency for International Development (USAID) (2007).* http://pdf.usaid.gov/pdf_docs/PNADJ990.pdf

When Disaster Strikes: A Guide to Assessing Seed System Security Seed security assessment tool to encourage more targeted strategies for addressing acute and chronic seed insecurity. *Catholic Relief Services (2008). Louise Sperling.* http://www.crsprogramquality.org/publications/2011/1/13/when-disaster-strikes.html

Seed Security: Advice for Practitioners Ten practice briefs offer advice on how to sustain and strengthen seed systems during disaster response and recovery periods. *International Center for Tropical Agriculture and CRS, with CARE Norway (2011).* http://www.crsprogramquality.org/publications/2011/1/12/seed-aid-for-seed-security.html

Seed Fairs and Vouchers: A Manual for Seed-Based Agricultural Recovery in Africa The manual provides an overview of seed systems and their components, and describes how to plan and implement the seed voucher/seed fair approach. *Catholic Relief Services (2002). In collaboration with Overseas Development Institute and International Crops Research Institute for the Semi-Arid Tropics.* http://www.crsprogramquality.org/publications/2011/1/12/seed-vouchers-and-fairs.html

The Livelihood Assessment Tool kit: Analysing and responding to the impact of disasters on the livelihoods of people A tool kit designed to support analysis and action on livelihoods post-disaster. *FAO, International Labor Organization (ILO) (2009).* http://www.fao.org/fileadmin/templates/tc/tce/pdf/LAT_Brochure_LoRes.pdf

Livelihoods and Climate Change: Combining disaster risk reduction, natural resource management and climate change adaptation in a new approach to the reduction of vulnerability and poverty A framework for researchers, policy makers and community groups seeking to take action on adaptation. *IUCN, Stockholm Environment Institute (SEI), IISD, Inter Co operation (2003).* http://www.iisd.org/pdf/2003/natres_livelihoods_cc.pdf

Adaptation toolkit: Integrating Adaptation to Climate Change into Secure Livelihoods A tool kit designed to support the integration of climate change and disasters into livelihoods work. *Christian Aid (2010).* http://unfccc.int/files/adaptation/application/pdf/christianaid_ap_update_sep_09_toolkit_6_sp.pdf

"Climate-Smart" Agriculture: Policies, Practices and Financing for Food Security, Adaptation and Mitigation An approach that examines key technical, institutional, policy and financial responses required to achieve climate smart agriculture. *FAO (2010).* http://www.fao.org/docrep/013/i1881e/i1881e00.pdf

TNA Guidebook Series: Technologies for Climate Change Adaptation — Agriculture Sector Adaptation technologies for the agriculture sector. *UNEP Risø Centre on Energy, Climate and Sustainable Development (2011). R. Clements, J. Haggar, A. Quezada, J. Torres, X. Zhu (ed).* http://tech-action.org/Guidebooks/TNA_Guidebook_AdaptationAgriculture.pdf

Practitioners' Guide to Household Economy Approach (HEA) A livelihoods-based framework designed to provide a clear and accurate representation of the internal workings of household economies. *RHVP, FEG, Save the Children (n.d.). M. Lawrence, P. Holzmann, M. O'Donnell, L. Adams, J. Holt, L. Hammond, A. Duffield, T. Boudreau (ed).* http://www.feg-consulting.com/resource/practitioners-guide-to-hea

4.3 Key sectors/ Natural Resource Management (NRM)

Consultation Workshop on Ecosystem-based Disaster Risk Reduction for Sustainable Development: Tools for integrating risk, climate projections and ecosystem data Guidance on hazard, risk and vulnerability mapping as tools for project planning. *Partnership for Environment and Disaster Risk Reduction (PEDRR) (n.d.).* http://cmsdata.iucn.org/downloads/5_2_tools_for_integrating_risk__climate_projections_and_ecosystem_data_2.pdf

Ecosystem Services: A Guide for Decision Makers List of ecosystem services. *WRI (2008). J. Ranganathan, C. Raudsepp Hearne, N. Lucas, F. Irwin, M. Zurek, K. Bennett, N. Ash, P. West.* http://pdf.wri.org/ecosystem_services_guide_for_decisionmakers.pdf

Integrating Community and Ecosystem-Based Approaches in Climate Change Adaptation Responses A conceptual framework for an approach to adaptation, which empowers local communities to manage ecosystems under resilient governance arrangements that can provide the ecosystem services on which they depend. *Ecosystems, Livelihoods and Adaptation Network (ELAN) (n.d.). P. Girot, C. Ehrhart, J. Oglethorpe.* http://www.careclimatechange.org/files/adaptation/ELAN_IntegratedApproach_150412.pdf

Ecosystem-based Adaptation: a natural response to climate change Provides a framework for EbA and its role in sustainable development. *IUCN (2009). A. Colls, N. Ash, N. Ikkala.* http://data.iucn.org/dbtw-wpd/edocs/2009-049.pdf p. 14 - Principles of effective ecosystem-based adaptation

A Short History of Farmer Managed Natural Regeneration: The Niger Experience. An ECHO Technical Note A practical programming approach to the regeneration of trees by communities with the aim of impacting water retention, livelihood enhancement, agricultural production and reducing soil erosion. *World Vision, Serving in Mission (SIM), ECHO (2010). T. Rinaudo.* http://www.echonet.org/data/sites/2/Documents/OuagaForum2010/FarmerManagedNaturalRegeneration.pdf

Guidelines for Rapid Environmental Impact Assessment in Disasters Guidance on conducting a rapid Environmental Impact Assessment. *Benfield Hazard Research Centre, University College London and CARE International (2005). C. Kelly.* http://www.preventionweb.net/files/8267_bhrcgen30apr1.pdf

Environmental Impact Assessment Environmental impact assessment training resources. *United Nations Environmental Programme.* http://www.unep.ch/etb/publications/envilmpAsse.php

Mainstreaming Adaptation to Climate Change in Agriculture and Natural Resources Management Projects Guidance for lessons learned, best practices, recommendations, and useful resources for integrating climate change risk management and adaptation to climate change in development projects. *The World Bank (2010). G. Gambarelli, A. Bucher.* http://climatechange.worldbank.org/ content/mainstreaming-adaptation-climate-change-agriculture-and-natural-resources-management-project

4.4 Key sectors/ Water, sanitation and hygiene (WASH)

Training Manual: Hydro climatic Disasters in Water Resources Management A manual that explains the links between Integrated Water Resources Management (IWRM) and water-related disasters. *Cap-Net UNDP, Nile IWRM-Net, UNISDR, United Nations Office of Humanitarian Coordination (UNOCHA) (2009).* http://www.unisdr.org/files/10358_ManualforHydroclimaticDisastersinWa.pdf

Water Safety Plan Manual: Step-by-step risk management for drinking-water suppliers Guidance to facilitate WSP development focusing on organized water supplies managed by a water utility or similar entity. *WHO, International Water Association (IWA) (2009). J. Bartram, L. Corrales, A. Davison, D. Deere, D. Drury, B. Gordon, G. Howard, A. Rinehold, M. Stevens.* http://www.preventionweb.net/files/8367_9789241562638eng1.pdf

Vision 2030: The resilience of water supply and sanitation in the face of climate change Website containing resources related to a study of climate change, drinking water and sanitation services. *WHO (2010).* http://www.who.int/water_sanitation_health/publications/9789241598422_cdrom/en/index.html

4.5 Key sectors/ Education

Inter-Agency Network for Education in Emergencies Toolkit (INEE) A toolkit to guide humanitarian aid workers, government officials and educationalists working in the field of education in emergencies. *The Inter-Agency Network for Education in Emergencies.* http://toolkit.ineesite.org/toolkit/Home.php

Child-led disaster risk reduction: a practical guide A guide aimed at practitioners working with children to provide them with examples and ideas to help them enable children to lead the process of disaster risk reduction. *Save the Children (Sweden) (2007). L. Benson, J. Bugge.* http://www.eldis.org/go/topics/resource-guides/aid/key-issues/disaster-risk-reduction/education-and-drr&id=38480&type=Document

Child-Centred Disaster Risk Reduction Toolkit A tool kit that supports practitioners to undertake PCVAs with children; planning, monitoring and evaluation of child-centered disaster risk reduction programs; action planning; and advocacy. *Plan International (2010).* http://www.childreninachangingclimate.org/library_page. htm?metadata_value=Child-Centred DRR Toolkit&wildmeta_value=Child-Centred DRR Toolkit

Knowledge, Attitudes and Practices for Risk Education: how to implement KAP surveys Guidance on how to design and implement KAP for risk education. *Handicap International (2009). F. Goutille.* http://www.handicap-international.org.uk/Resources/ Handicap%20International/PDF%20Documents/HI%20Associations/KAPRiskEducation_2009.pdf

Convention on the Rights of the Child (CRC) A legally binding international instrument that sets out the basic human rights of children everywhere. *UNICEF (1990).* Summary document: http://www.unicef.org/crc/files/Rights_overview.pdf Full document: http://www.coe.int/t/dg3/children/participation/CRC-C-GC-12.pdf

Disaster risk reduction begins at School. 2006-2007 World Disaster Reduction Campaign Descriptions of good practices from around the world in school-based DRR. *UNISDR, United Educational and Scientific Organization (UNESCO) (n.d.).* http://www.unisdr.org/we/inform/publications/2105

Children in a Changing Climate A coalition of organizations that share knowledge, coordinate activities and work with children and young people to highlight the importance of child-centered disaster risk reduction and climate change prevention and adaptation. *IDS, Plan, Save the Children, UNICEF, World Vision (2007).* www.childreninachangingclimate.org/

Guidance Notes on Safer School Construction A framework of guiding principles and general steps to support disaster-resilient construction and retrofitting of school buildings. *Inter-Agency Network for Education in Emergencies (INEE), World Bank, UNISDR (2009).* http://www.gfdrr.org/gfdrr/sites/gfdrr.org/files/publication/Guidance_Notes_Safe_ Schools.pdf

Climate Change Education Website containing resources on education for sustainable development. *Education for Sustainable Development.* http://educationforsustainabledevelopment.com/blog/?cat=11

4.6 Key sectors/ Health

PDNA/RF Fast Facts Guidance Sheet Guidance sheets for post-disaster assessments. *UNDP (2009).* http://www.recoveryplatform.org/assets/publication/PDNA/PDNA%20 guidance%20sheet.pdf

✱ **An Approach for Assessing Human Health Vulnerability and Public Health Interventions to Adapt to Climate Change** A resource that outlines steps in assessing vulnerability and capacity in the health sector. *Research Mini-Monograph. K. L. Ebi, R. S. Kovats, B.Menne. Environmental Health Perspectives, Vol 114, No 12, December 2006.* http://www.ncbi.nlm.nih.gov/pmc/articles/PMC1764166/pdf/ehp0114-001930.pdf

Cholera Outbreak Guidelines: Preparedness, prevention and control A step-by-step guide to inform cholera outbreak interventions and ensure public health programs that are rapid, community-based, well-tailored, and gender and diversity aware. *Oxfam GB (2012). E. Lamond, J. Kinyanjui.* http://policy-practice.oxfam.org.uk/publications/cholera-outbreak-guidelines-preparedness-prevention-and-control-237172

4.7 Key sectors/ Protection

Protection: An ALNAP guide for humanitarian agencies Advice and insights to humanitarian practitioners involved in providing safety and protecting vulnerable people in war and disaster. *Active Learning Network for Accountability and Performance, Overseas Development Institute (2005). H. Slim, A. Bonwick.* http://www.alnap.org/pool/files/alnap-protection-guide.pdf

5.1 Key contexts/ Conflict

Integrating conflict and disaster risk reduction into education sector planning: Guidance Notes for Educational Planners Guidance notes to support educational planners integrate CCA/DRR into their planning processes. *Global Education Cluster, UNESCO, International Institute for Educational Policy (IIEP), UNICEF (2011).* http://toolkit.ineesite.org/toolkit/INEEcms/uploads/1096/IIEP_Guidance_notes_EiE_EN.pdf

The Do No Harm Handbook: The Framework for Analyzing the Impact of Assistance on Conflict Essential information, key steps and lessons learnt on the 'do no harm' methodology. *Collaborative for Development Action (CDA) Collaborative Learning Projects (2004).* http://www.cdainc.com/dnh/docs/DoNoHarmHandbook.pdf

Guidance for designing, monitoring and evaluating peacebuilding projects: using theories of change Methods to monitor and evaluate peacebuilding projects; this document provides guidance for designing, monitoring and evaluating peacebuilding projecst: using theories of change. The main audiences for this guide are conflict transformation and peacebuilding practitioners, non-governmental organizations (NGOs) and donor agencies. Other actors in the conflict transformation and peacebuilding field may also find it useful. *CARE International and International Alert (2012).* http://www.careinternational.org.uk/research-centre/conflict-and-peacebuilding/227-guidance-for-designing-monitoring-and-evaluating-peacebuilding-projects-using-theories-of-change

Making Sense of Turbulent Contexts: Analysis Tools for Humanitarian Actors A macro-context tool for the analysis of the history, actor groups, political economy, and strategic needs of conflict contexts. *World Vision International (2003). S. Jackson with S. Calthrop.* http://www.conflictsensitivity.org/node/85

Consensus Building with Participatory Action Plan Development A consensus-building tool that seeks to identify and then solve environmental or livelihoods problems with community support and input. *Practical Action (2011). A. Taha, R. Lewins, S. Coupe, B. Peacocke.* http://practicalaction.org/consensus-building-with-participatory-action-plan-development

Political economy analysis Analysis that focuses on developing an understanding of the political and the economic drivers of conflict, and the relative power, exclusion and vulnerability of different groups over time. *Governance and Social Development Resource Centre, University of Birmingham.* http://www.gsdrc.org/go/topic-guides/political-economy-analysis/tools-for-political-economy-analysis

Disaster-Conflict Interface: Comparative experiences A comparative analysis of tendencies and experiences that stem from the relationship between disasters and conflict. *Bureau for Crisis Prevention and Recovery, UNDP (2011).* http://www.undp.org/content/dam/undp/library/crisis%20prevention/DisasterConflict72p.pdf

5.2 Key contexts/ Early recovery

Guidance Note on Recovery: Climate Change Guidance on early recovery and climate change. *UNISDR, UNDP, International Recovery Platform (n.d.).* www.unisdr.org/we/inform/publications/16769

Early Recovery Cluster Overview Website containing information, tools and resources related to early recovery. *OneResponse, Cluster Working Group on Early Recovery, UNDP.* http://oneresponse.info/GlobalClusters/Early%20Recovery/Pages/default.aspx

5.3 Key contexts/ Urban

Earthquakes and Megacities Initiative (EMI) An international scientific initiative established as a not-for-profit organization to advance urban risk reduction policy, knowledge, and practice in megacities and fast-growing metropolises. *EMI.* http://www.emi-megacities.org/home/

Climate Resilient Cities: A Primer on Reducing Vulnerabilities to Disasters A guide for local governments to better understand the concepts and consequences of climate change; how climate change consequences contribute to urban vulnerabilities; and what is being done by city governments around the world to engage in learning, capacity building, and capital investment programs for building resilient communities. *The World Bank (2009). N. Prasad, F. Ranghieri, Fatima Shah, Z. Trohanis, E. Kessler, R. Sinha.* http://siteresources.worldbank.org/INTEAPREGTOPURBDEV/Resources/Primer_e_book.pdf

The 10 Essentials for Making Cities Resilient *A 10-point checklist and the building block for disaster risk reduction, developed in line with the five priorities of the HFA. UNISDR (2012).* http://www.unisdr.org/campaign/resilientcities/toolkit/essentials

How to make cities more resilient: a handbook for local government leaders A handbook that provides mayors, governors, councilors and other local government leaders with a generic framework for risk reduction and points to good practices and tools that are already being applied in cities for that purpose. *UNISDR (2012).* http://www.unisdr.org/campaign/resilientcities/toolkit//handbook

Local Government Self-Assessment Tool (LGSAT) The Local Government Self-Assessment Tool (LGSAT) provides key questions and measurements against The 10 Essentials for Making Cities Resilient and builds upon the priorities and national indicators of the HFA. *UNISDR (2012).* http://www.unisdr.org/campaign/resilientcities/toolkit/howto

Planning for Climate Change: A Strategic, Values-based Approach for Urban Planners A guide to developing a values-based, strategic, participatory approach to incorporating climate change in urban planning and development. *UN-Habitat (2011).* http://www.unhabitat.org/downloads/docs/PFCC-14-03-11.pdf

OCHA and slow-onset emergencies. OCHA Occasional Policy Briefing Series No. 6 A policy briefing paper that provides recommendations of how national and international humanitarian partners can prepare for and respond to slow-onset disasters. *UNOCHA Policy and Development Studies Branch (2011).* http://reliefweb.int/sites/reliefweb.int/files/resources/report_36.pdf

From food crisis to fair trade: Livelihoods analysis, protection and support in emergencies Practical guidance on livelihoods programming in emergencies. *Emergency Nutrition Network, Oxfam (2006). S. Jaspars.* http://www.ennonline.net/pool/files/ife/supplement27.pdf

The Household Economy Approach: A Resource Manual for Practitioners A manual that serves as both an introduction for field workers to the HEA and a reference for those who have experience of this approach. *Save the Children (2000). J. Seaman, P. Clarke, T. Boudreau, J. Holt.* http://www.savethechildren.org.uk/resources/online-library/household-economy-approach-resource-manual-practitioners

5.4 Key contexts/ Slow-onset disasters

The Coping Strategies Index: Field Methods Manual The Coping Strategies Index (CSI) is an indicator of household food security, and correlates well with more complex measures of food security. *CARE International, World Food Programme (2003). D. Maxwell, B. Watkins, R. Wheeler, G. Collins.* http://www.fao.org/crisisandhunger/root/pdf/cop_strat.pdf

Slow-onset disasters: drought and food and livelihoods insecurity. Learning from previous relief and recovery responses A synthesis of key lessons learnt from evaluations of relief and recovery responses to past slow-onset disasters – particularly drought, and food and livelihoods insecurity. *Active Learning Network for Accountability and Performance (ALNAP), ProVention Consortium (n.d.).* http://www.alnap.org/pool/files/ALNAP-ProVention_lessons_on_slow-onset_disasters.pdf

6.1 Enabling environment/ Governance

Powercube An online resource for understanding power relations in efforts to bring about social change. *IDS.* http://www.powercube.net/

From Vulnerability to Resilience: A framework for analysis and action to build community resilience A framework for analysis and action aimed at reducing vulnerability and strengthening the resilience of individuals, households, and communities. *Practical Action Publishing (2011). K. Pasteur.* http://practicalaction.org/media/view/9654

Innovation and good practice in DRR Governance in Asia: Lessons Learnt ADPC presentation on innovation and good practice in DRR governance in Asia. *Asia Disaster Preparedness Centre (ADPC) (2007).* http://www.adrc.asia/acdr/2007astana/Presentations/Day1_Part1/Part1_ADPC.pdf

Disaster Risk Reduction, Governance and Mainstreaming Working paper on the mainstreaming of DRR in local and national government. *UNDP Bureau for Crisis Prevention and Recovery (2010).* http://www.undp.org.cu/crmi/docs/undp-drrbrief4gov-in-2010-en.pdf

Governance Programming Framework (GPF) A comprehensive framework for integrating governance issues in programs. *CARE International (n.d)*. http://governance.care2share.wikispaces.net/Governance+Programming+Guide

6.2 Enabling environment/ Advocacy

A Practical Guide to Advocacy for Disaster Risk Reduction A Guide designed to further enhance the skills, knowledge and proficiency of disaster risk reduction practitioners to advocate and communicate on disaster risk reduction. *IFRC (2009)*. http://www.preventionweb.net/english/professional/publications/v.php?id=16348

Advocacy Tools and Guidelines: Promoting Policy Change Tools and guidelines to help program managers acquire the essential skills to help become effective advocates. *CARE International (2001). S. Sprechmann, E. Pelton.* http://www.care.org/getinvolved/advocacy/tools.asp

Guidebook on Advocacy - Integrating CBDRM into Local Government Policy and Programming Guidance on how to integrate community-based disaster risk management into local government policy and practice. *ADPC, European Commission, United Nations Economic and Social Commission for Asia and the Pacific (UNESCAP) (2006). I. Haider Butt.* http://www.adpc.net/pdrsea/pubs/advocacyfull.pdf

Glossary

Adaptive capacity
The ability of a system (individual or community) to adjust to climate change (including climate variability and extremes) to moderate potential damages, to take advantage of opportunities, or to cope with the consequences (IPCC, 2000).

Agriculture
The science or practice of farming, including cultivation of the soil for the growing of crops and the rearing of animals to provide food, wool, and other products (*Oxford English Dictionary, n.d.*).

Biodiversity
The variability among living organisms within species, between species, and between organisms. Biodiversity is not itself an ecosystem service, but rather supports the supply of all services (WRI, 2009).

Building back better
Post-disaster recovery processes and interventions that not only restore what existed previously, but go beyond, seizing the moral, political, managerial, and financial opportunities the crisis has offered governments to set communities on a better and safer development path. (Office of the UN Secretary-General's Special Envoy for Tsunami Recovery, 2006).

Capacity
The combination of all the strengths, attributes and resources available within a community, society or organization that can be used to achieve agreed goals (UNISDR, 2009). Note: Capacity may include infrastructure and physical means, institutions, societal coping abilities, as well as human knowledge, skills and collective attributes such as social relationships, leadership and management.

Child-centered disaster risk reduction
Disaster risk reduction that places children at the heart of its activities, recognizes the specific vulnerabilities children face from disasters, focuses on children's needs and rights, as well as supports and draws on their participation in identifying and addressing those needs and rights (Save the Children, 2011).

Civil society
The wide array of non-governmental and not-for-profit organizations that have a presence in public life, expressing the interests and values of their members or others, based on ethical, cultural, political, scientific, religious or philanthropic considerations. Civil society organizations (CSO) therefore refer to a wide of array of organizations: community groups, non-governmental organizations (NGOs), labor unions, indigenous groups, charitable organizations, faith-based organizations, professional associations, and foundations (The World Bank, n.d.).

Climate change
A change in the climate that persists for decades or longer, arising from natural causes or human activity (IPCC, 2000).

Climate change adaptation
The adjustment in natural or human systems in response to actual or expected climatic stimuli or their effects, which moderates harm or exploits beneficial opportunities (IPCC, 2000). Or, a) Adapting development to gradual changes in average temperature, sea-level and precipitation; and, b) reducing and managing the risks associated with more frequent, severe and unpredictable extreme weather events (UNISDR, n.d.)

Climate change effects

Changes in the climate as a result of excessive emissions of greenhouse gas, including: temperature increases on land and at sea; sea-level rise; the melting of glaciers and ice caps; and changing and irregular rainfall patterns.

Climate sensitivity

A measure of how responsive the temperature of the climate system is to a change in the radiative forcing (most commonly carbon dioxide). The climate sensitivity specifically due to carbon dioxide is often expressed as the temperature change in degrees Celsius associated with a doubling of the concentration of carbon dioxide in Earth's atmosphere (IPCC, 2001).

Climate variability

Variations in the mean state and other statistics (such as standard deviations, the occurrence of extremes, etc.) of the climate on all spatial and temporal scales beyond that of individual weather events. Variability may be due to natural internal processes within the climate system (internal variability), or to variations in natural or anthropogenic external forcing (external variability) (IPCC, 2000)

Conflict

A state of open, often prolonged fighting; a battle or war (Free Dictionary, n.d.). Note: Conflict can apply both to open fighting between hostile groups and to a struggle between opposing forces.

Conflict (latent)

Latent conflict exists whenever individuals, groups, organizations, or nations have differences that bother one or the other, but those differences are not great enough to cause one side to act to alter the situation (Wehr, 1975). Note: Latent conflict is often rooted in longstanding economic inequality, or in groups' unequal access to political power. The government may be unresponsive to the needs of a minority or lower-power group. Strong value or status differences may exist. Any of these issues could emerge as an open conflict after a triggering event.

Contingency planning

A management process that analyses specific potential events or emerging situations that might threaten society or the environment and establishes arrangements in advance to enable timely, effective and appropriate responses to such events and situations (UNISDR, 2009).

Coping Strategies Index (CSI)

An indicator of household food security, which correlates well with more complex measures of food security. A series of questions, about how households manage to cope with a shortfall in food, results in a simple numeric score. In its simplest form, monitoring changes in the CSI score indicates whether household food security status is declining or improving (Maxwell et al, 2003).

Deforestation

The conversion of forest to another land use or the long-term reduction of tree canopy cover below a 10 percent threshold. Deforestation implies the long-term or permanent loss of forest cover and its transformation into another land use (University of Michigan, 2011).

Desertification

Land degradation in arid, semi-arid, and dry sub-humid areas resulting from factors including climatic variations and human activities (IPCC, 2000).

Disaster

A serious disruption of the functioning of a community or a society involving widespread human, material, economic or environmental losses and impacts, which exceeds the ability of the affected community or society to cope using its own resources (UNISDR, 2009). Note: Disasters are often described as a result of the combination of: the exposure to a hazard; the conditions of vulnerability that are present; and insufficient capacity or measures to reduce or cope with the potential negative consequences. Disaster impacts may include loss of life, injury, disease and other negative effects on human physical, mental and social wellbeing, together with damage to property, destruction of assets, loss of services, social and economic disruption and environmental degradation.

Disaster risk

The potential disaster losses, in lives, health status, livelihoods, assets and services, which could occur to a particular community or a society over some specified future time period (UNISDR, 2009).

Disaster risk reduction

The concept and practice of reducing disaster risks through systematic efforts to analyze and manage the causal factors of disasters, including through reduced exposure to hazards, lessened vulnerability of people and property, wise management of land and the environment, and improved preparedness for adverse events (UNISDR, 2009).

Early recovery

After a disaster, early recovery is about shifting the focus from saving lives to restoring livelihoods. Early recovery interventions seek to stabilize the economic, governance, human security and social equity situation. Early recovery interventions also seek to integrate risk reduction at the very early stages of the response to a specific crisis; and to lay the foundations for longer-term reconstruction (UNISDR, 2009).

Early warning system

The set of capacities needed to generate and disseminate timely and meaningful warning information to enable individuals, communities and organizations threatened by a hazard to prepare and to act appropriately and in sufficient time to reduce the possibility of harm or loss (UNISDR, 2009). Note: This definition encompasses the range of factors necessary to achieve effective responses to warnings. A people-centered early warning system necessarily comprises four key elements: knowledge of the risks; monitoring, analysis and forecasting of the hazards; communication or dissemination of alerts and warnings; and local capabilities to respond to the warnings received.

Ecosystem-based adaptation

Ecosystem-based adaptation integrates the use of biodiversity and ecosystem services into an overall strategy to help people adapt to the adverse impacts of climate change. It includes the sustainable management, conservation and restoration of ecosystems to provide services that help people adapt to both current climate variability, and climate change (IUCN, 2009).

Ecosystem services

The benefits that people and communities derive from ecosystems. These include provisioning services, such as food and water; regulating services, such as flood and disease control; cultural services, such as spiritual, recreational, and cultural benefits; and supporting services, such as nutrient cycling that maintain the conditions for life on Earth (Millennium Ecosystem Assessment, 2005).

Emergency Market Mapping Assessment/Analysis (EMMA)

EMMA is a rapid market analysis designed to be used in the first two to three weeks of a sudden onset crisis. Its rationale is that a better understanding of the most critical markets in an emergency situation enables decision makers (i.e. donors, NGOs, government, other humanitarian actors) to consider a broader range of responses. It is not intended to replace existing emergency assessments, or more thorough household and economic analyses such as the Household Economy Approach, but instead should add to the body of knowledge after a crisis.

Environmental degradation

The reduction of the capacity of the environment to meet social and ecological objectives and needs (UNISDR, 2009). Note: Degradation of the environment can alter the frequency and intensity of natural hazards and increase the vulnerability of communities. The types of human-induced degradation include land misuse; soil erosion and loss; desertification; wild fires; loss of biodiversity; deforestation; mangrove destruction; land, water and air pollution; climate change; sea-level rise; and ozone depletion.

Environmental impact assessment

Process by which the environmental consequences of a proposed project or program are evaluated, undertaken as an integral part of planning and decision-making processes with a view to limiting or reducing the adverse impacts of the project or program (UNISDR, 2009).

Exposure

Measures of exposure can include the number of people or types of assets in an area. These can be combined with the specific vulnerability of the exposed elements to any particular hazard to estimate the quantitative risks associated with that hazard in the area of interest (UNISDR, 2009). Note: Exposure generally means physically being in, or depending on, assets, systems, institutions or other people that are in the area affected by the hazard or climatic phenomenon.

Farmer Managed Natural Regeneration (FMNR)

FMNR is based on the regeneration of native trees and shrubs from mature root systems of previously cleared desert shrubs and trees. Regeneration techniques are used in agricultural cropland and to manage trees as part of a farm enterprise. By selectively protecting and pruning a number of these saplings in the fields, they regenerate into trees rapidly and provide a sustainable timber supply. Fallen leaves provide nutrients and offer moisture retention to the exhausted soils. Other benefits include their use as animal fodder, for wild foods and medicines, and as a harbour for birds and lizards that feed on crop pests.

Food insecurity

A situation that exists when people lack secure access to sufficient amounts of safe and nutritious food for normal growth and development and an active and healthy life. It may be caused by the unavailability of food, insufficient purchasing power, inappropriate distribution, or inadequate use of food at the household level. Food insecurity may be chronic, seasonal, or transitory (IPCC, 2000).

Fossil fuels

Carbon-based fuels from fossil carbon deposits, including coal, oil, and natural gas (IPCC, 2000).

Gender

The social differences between women and men, girls and boys, throughout the life cycle. These gender differences are learned, and though deeply rooted in every culture, are changeable over time, and have wide variations both within and between cultures. 'Gender', along with other aspects of social identity such as class and race, determines the roles, power, and access to resources for women and men in any culture (Oxfam GB, 2010).

Gender equality
The equal enjoyment by women, girls, boys, and men of rights, opportunities, resources, and rewards; an equal say in the development process; and the same level of dignity and respect. Equality does not mean that women and men are the same, but that they have the same power to make choices, and the same opportunities to act on those choices (Oxfam GB, 2010).

Gender mainstreaming
Ensuring that gender perspectives and attention to the goal of gender equality are central to all activities—policy development, research, advocacy/ dialogue, legislation, resource allocation, and planning, implementation and monitoring of programmes and projects (UN Women, 2011).

Governance
The exercise of political, economic and administrative authority in the management of a country's affairs at all levels. It comprises mechanisms, processes and institutions through which citizens and groups articulate their interests, exercise their legal rights, meet their obligations and mediate their differences. Governance encompasses, but also transcends, the state. It encompasses all relevant groups, including the private sector and civil society organizations (UNDP, 1997).

Greenhouse gases
Gaseous constituents of the atmosphere, both natural and caused by human activity, that absorb and emit radiation at specific wavelengths within the spectrum of infrared radiation emitted by the Earth's surface, the atmosphere, and clouds (IPCC, 2000). Note: The main greenhouse gases (GHG) are water vapor, carbon dioxide, nitrous oxide, methane and ozone.

Hazard
A dangerous phenomenon, event (e.g. flood, cyclone, earthquake), human activity (e.g. civil conflict) or condition that may cause loss of life, injury or other health impacts, property damage, loss of livelihoods and services, social and economic disruption, or environmental damage. Hazards can be single, sequential or combined in origin and effects. Each hazard is characterized by its location, intensity, frequency and probability. Understanding the nature and likelihood of such hazards is critical to individual and community safety and security (UNISDR, 2009).

Heat island
A zone, within an urban area, characterized by ambient temperatures higher than those of the surrounding area because of the absorption of solar energy by materials like asphalt (IPCC, 2000).

Information, Education and Communication (IEC) materials
IEC materials are intended to support awareness raising, knowledge and behaviour change within the target audience. Materials include: printed materials (e.g. brochures, posters, advertisements), mass media (e.g. television, radio, print), giveaways (e.g. t-shirts, key chains, caps) and community events. Materials should be culturally sensitive and acceptable to the target audience, and should involve the active participation of the target audience in their development.

Knowledge, Attitudes and Practices (KAP) Survey
KAP studies tell us what people know about certain things, how they feel, and how they behave. Whereas social surveys may cover a wide range of social values and activities, KAP

studies focus specifically on the knowledge, attitudes and practices (behaviours) for a certain topic. *Knowledge* refers to the understanding of a community of a particular topic. *Attitude* refers to their feelings toward this subject, as well as any preconceived ideas they may have towards it. *Practice* refers to the ways in which they demonstrate their knowledge and attitudes through their actions (FAO, n.d.).

Land-use change

A change in the use or management of land by humans, which may lead to a change in land cover. Land cover and land-use change may have an impact on climate, locally or globally (IPCC, 2000).

Livelihood

A livelihood comprises the resources (including skills, technology and organizations) and activities required to make a living and have a good quality of life (Pasteur, 2011).

Mal-adaptation

Actions that increase vulnerability to climate change. This includes making development or investment decisions while neglecting the actual or potential impacts of both climate variability and longer-term climate change (Burton, 1998).

Mitigation (climate change-related)

Measures to reduce greenhouse gas emissions (UNISDR, 2009).

Mitigation (disaster-related)

The lessening or limitation of the adverse impacts of hazards and related disasters (UNISDR, 2009). Note: The adverse impacts of hazards often cannot be prevented fully, but their scale or severity can be substantially lessened by various strategies and actions. Mitigation measures encompass engineering techniques and hazard-resistant construction as well as improved environmental policies and public awareness.

Monitoring, evaluation and learning (MEL)

Monitoring is the systematic assessment of a program's performance over time. It involves the ongoing collection and review of data to provide program managers and other stakeholders with indications of progress against program plans and towards program objectives (Oxfam GB, n.d). *Evaluations* complement ongoing monitoring activities by providing more in-depth, objective assessments of the relevance, efficiency, effectiveness, impact and sustainability of programs at a particular point in time (Oxfam GB, n.d). *Learning* is the result of effective monitoring and evaluation and shares the lessons learned from programs within organizations and externally.

Natural Resource Management (NRM)

The management of natural resources to bring into being development that is economically viable, socially beneficial, and ecologically sustainable (Hughes, 2001).

'No-regrets' adaptation

Options or measures that can be justified (and will be effective) under all plausible future climate change scenarios. 'No-regrets' adaptation is not affected by uncertainties related to future climate change because it helps address problems associated with current climate variability, while at the same time, builds adaptive capacity for future climate change. An example of a no-regret option would be enhancing provision and dissemination of climate information as well as access to early warning systems by local communities living in flood and/or drought prone areas (The World Bank, n.d.).

Participatory Capacity and Vulnerability Analysis (PCVA)

An analytical and planning process (and associated tool of the same name), used originally to facilitate community-led assessment of local disaster risk. The process uses a participatory approach and techniques to develop understanding and capture data about vulnerability and exposure to hazards, and to prioritize actions to reduce disaster risk. PCVA and its variations are increasingly used for broader analysis and development planning processes, including for climate change adaptation (Authors' definition).

Post-Disaster Needs Assessment and Recovery Framework (PDNA/RF)

A government-led exercise that pulls together information into a single, consolidated report detailing information on the physical impacts of a disaster, the economic value of the damages and losses, the human impacts as experienced by affected populations, and related early and long-term recovery needs and priorities. (UNDP, 1997).

Preparedness

The knowledge and capacities developed by governments, professional response and recovery organizations, communities and individuals to effectively anticipate, respond to, and recover from, the impacts of likely, imminent or current hazard events or conditions (UNISDR, 2009). Note: Preparedness action is carried out within the context of disaster risk management and aims to build the capacities needed to efficiently manage all types of emergencies and achieve orderly transitions, from response through to sustained recovery. Preparedness is based on a sound analysis of disaster risks and good linkages with early warning systems, and includes such activities as contingency planning; stockpiling of equipment and supplies; the development of arrangements for coordination, evacuation and public information; and associated training and field exercises.

Prevention

The outright avoidance of adverse impacts of hazards and related disasters (UNISDR, 2009). Note: Prevention (i.e. disaster prevention) expresses the concept and intention to completely avoid potential adverse impacts through action taken in advance. Examples include dams or embankments that eliminate flood risks, land-use regulations that do not permit any settlement in high-risk zones, and seismic engineering designs that ensure the survival and function of a critical building in an earthquake.

Protection

All activities, aimed at obtaining full respect for the rights of the individual in accordance with the letter and the spirit of the relevant bodies of law (i.e. human rights, humanitarian and refugee law). Human rights and humanitarian actors shall conduct these activities impartially and not on the basis of race, national or ethnic origin, language or gender (ICRC, 1999).

Resilience

Resilience refers to the capacity of an individual, household, population group or system to anticipate, absorb, and recover from hazards and/or effects of climate change and other shocks and stresses[G] without compromising (and potentially enhancing) its long-term prospects.
Note: The term 'resilience' is the subject of numerous studies, and its definition is likely to be modified repeatedly in the near future. The definition used in this guide has been adapted from UNISDR Terminology 2009 and the DFID working definition.
Resilience is not a fixed end state, but is a dynamic set of conditions and processes. Underpinning resilience is the need for better analysis of risk at different spatial and temporal levels, and for analysis to be monitored and updated to inform and enhance programming.

Rights-based approach

A framework that integrates the norms, principles, standards and goals of the international human rights system into the plans and processes of development. It is characterized by methods and activities that link the human rights system and its inherent notion of power and struggle with development (Danish Institute for Human Rights, 2007). Note: A rights-based approach recognizes the rights of all human beings to realize their potential, and to have the opportunity to live free of poverty in a secure and more equitable world. This includes the right to: life and security; to a sustainable livelihood; to be heard; to have an identity; and to have access to basic social services.

Risk

The combination of the probability of an event and its negative consequences (UNISDR, 2009).

Salinization

The accumulation of salts in soils (IPCC, 2000).

Saltwater intrusion

Displacement of fresh surface water or groundwater by the advance of saltwater due to its greater density, usually in coastal and estuarine areas (IPCC, 2000).

Shock

A natural or human-made hazard that, when it occurs, may cause loss of life, injury or other health impacts, property damage, loss of livelihoods and services, social and economic disruption, and environmental damage. For example, droughts, floods, earthquakes, volcanic eruptions, epidemics, windstorms, heavy precipitation, chemical spills, conflict[G], and others (*See also* hazard).

Slow-onset disaster

An emergency that does not emerge from a single, distinct event but one that emerges gradually, often based on a confluence of events (UNOCHA, 2011).

SMART indicators

An indicator that is **S**pecific, **M**easurable, **A**chievable in a cost effective way, **R**elevant for the program, and available in a **T**imely manner (European Commission, n.d.).

Stakeholder

Any party (individual or collective) that is actively involved in a process; has interests that may be positively or negatively affected by the performance or completion of the project, and is able to exert influence over the project, its deliverables or its participants (Project Management Institute, 1996).

Storm surge

The temporary increase, at a particular locality, in the height of the sea due to extreme weather conditions (low atmospheric pressure and/or strong winds) (IPCC, 2000).

Stress

Negative pressures that take place over time which constrain the ability of an individual, household, population group, asset or system, to reach its full potential. For example, changing seasonality, irregular rainfall patterns, sea-level rise, population increase, and/or other negative long-term trends.

Sustainable development

Development that meets the needs of the present without compromising the ability of future generations to meet their own needs (UNISDR, 2009).

Vulnerability

The characteristics and circumstances of a community, system, or asset, that make it susceptible to the damaging effects of climate change and other hazards. Vulnerability can be determined by the interplay between exposure and sensitivity to a range of interrelated social, economic, political, governance and environmental factors (Oxfam GB, 2010). Note: There are many aspects of vulnerability, arising from various physical, social, economic, and environmental factors. Examples may include poor design and construction of buildings, inadequate protection of assets, lack of public information and awareness, limited official recognition of risks and preparedness measures, and disregard for wise environmental management. Vulnerability varies significantly within a community and over time.

Water stress

A country is water-stressed if the available freshwater supply relative to water withdrawals acts as an important constraint on development. Withdrawals exceeding 20 percent of renewable water supply have been used as an indicator of water stress (IPCC, 2000).

Glossary references

Boesen, J.K. and Martin, T. (2007) *Applying a Rights-based Approach: An Inspirational Guide for Civil Society.* Copenhagen, Denmark: Danish Institute for Human Rights.

Burton, I. (1998) 'Adapting to Climate Change in the Context of National Economic Planning and Development', in Veit, P. (ed.) *Africa's Valuable Assets: A Reader in Natural Resource Management.* Washington, DC, USA: World Resources Institute.

European Commission: European Network for Rural Development (n.d.) 'FAQs > Indicators' for Rural Development Programs. Brussels, Belgium. Available at: http://enrd. ec.europa.eu/evaluation/faq/en/indicators.cfm

FAO (n.d.) 'Knowledge Attitude and Practice (KAP) Survey' [online] Available at: http:// www.fao.org/Participation/ft_more.jsp?ID=8468

TheFreeDictionary.com (n.d.). 'Conflict'. Huntingdon Valley, PA, USA: Farlex Inc. Available at: www.thefreedictionary.com/conflict

Hughes, D. M. (2001) 'Cadastral Politics: The Making of Community-Based Resource Management in Zimbabwe and Mozambique', *Development and Change*, Vol. 32, Issue 4, pp.741–768. The Hague, The Netherlands: International Institute of Social Studies.

ICRC (1999) *ICRC Ecogia Protection Seminars* (1996-2000). Geneva, Switzerland.

IPCC (2000) 'Glossary of Terms used in the IPCC Fourth Assessment Report WGII'. Geneva, Switzerland. Available at: www.ipcc.ch/publications_and_data/publications_and_data_ glossary.shtml

IPCC (2001) *Climate Change 2001.* Working Group III: Mitigation. Geneva, Switzerland. Available at: www.grida.no/publications/other/ipcc_tar/

IPCC (2007) *Climate Change 2007.* Working Group I: The Physical Science Basis. Geneva, Switzerland. Available at: www.ipcc.ch/publications_and_data/ar4/wg1/en/contents. html

IUCN (2009) *Ecosystem-based Adaptation: A natural response to climate change.* (Convention on Biological Diversity, Chapter 2. Gland, Switzerland.

Maxwell, D., Watkins, B., Wheeler, R., and Collins, G. (2003) The Coping Strategies Index: Field Method Manual, CARE and World Food Programme. Available at: http://www.fao. org/crisisandhunger/root/pdf/cop_strat.pdf

Millennium Ecosystem Assessment (2005) Ecosystems and Human Wellbeing: Synthesis. Washington, DC: Island Press. Available at: www.maweb.org/documents/document.356. aspx.pdf

Oxfam GB (n.d.) *Rough Guide to Monitoring and Evaluation.* Oxford, UK.

Oxfam GB (2010) *Gender, Disaster Risk Reduction, and Climate Change Adaptation: A Learning Companion.* Oxfam Disaster Risk Reduction and Climate Change Adaptation Resources. Oxford, UK.

Oxford English Dictionary 'Agriculture' [online] Available at: http://oxforddictionaries.com/ definition/english/agriculture

Pasteur, K. (2011) *From Vulnerability to Resilience: A framework for analysis and action to build community resilience.* Rugby, UK: Practical Action Publishing.

Pettengell, C. (2010) *Climate Change Adaptation: Enabling people living in poverty to adapt.* Oxford, UK: Oxfam International.

Project Management Institute (1996) *A Guide to the Project Management Body of Knowledge.* Newton Square, Pennsylvania, USA.

Save the Children International (2011) *Reducing Risks, Saving Lives: Save the Children's approach to Disaster Risk Reduction and Climate Change Adaptation.* London, UK.

The Sphere Handbook: Humanitarian Charter and Minimum Standards in Humanitarian Response, Rugby, UK: Practical Action Publishing.

UNDP (1997) *Governance for sustainable human development.* Division Bureau for Policy and Program Support. New York, USA.

UNISDR (n.d.) Briefing Note 03, *Strengthening climate change adaptation through effective disaster risk reduction.*

UNISDR (2009) *Terminology on Disaster Risk Reduction.* Geneva, Switzerland. Available at: www.unisdr.org/files/7817_UNISDRTerminologyEnglish.pdf

UNOCHA (2011) *OCHA and slow-onset emergencies.* Occasional Policy Briefing Series No. 6. Available at: http://ochanet.unocha.org/p/Documents/OCHA_OPB_SlowOnsetEmergencies190411.pdf

University of Michigan (2011) 'Global deforestation'. Ann Arbor, Michigan, USA. Available at: www.globalchange.umich.edu/globalchange2/current/lectures/deforest/deforest.html

UN Women (2001) Strategy for Promoting Gender Equality, New York. Available at: http://www.un.org/womenwatch/osagi/gendermainstreaming.htm

Wehr, P. (1975) 'Conflict Emergence' in *Online Training Program on Intractable Conflict.* Boulder, Colorado, USA: Conflict Research Consortium, University of Colorado. Available at: www.colorado.edu/conflict/peace/problem/cemerge.htm

WFP (2000) *Contingency Planning Guidelines.* Rome, Italy. Available at: www.fews.net/docs/special/1000284.pdf

World Bank (n.d.) 'Climate Change' [online] Available at: http://climatechange.worldbank.org/climatechange/content/note-6-identification-and-analysis-possible-adaptation-options

World Resources Institute (2009) Ecosystem Services Indicators Database. Washington, DC, USA. Available at: www.esindicators.org/glossary

Acronyms and abbreviations

ACCRA	Africa Climate Change Resilience Alliance (Made up of Oxfam GB, Overseas Development Institute, Save the Children, CARE International, and World Vision International. Funded by DFID and CDKN)
ADP	Area Development Program
ALNAP	Active Learning Network for Accountability and Performance
BMZ	[Germany] Federal Ministry for Economic Cooperation and Development
BNPB	Badan Nasional Penanggulangan Bencana (National Board for Disaster Management, Indonesia)
CAIT	Climate Analysis Indicators Tool
CAN-I	Climate Action Network International
CBA	Community-based Adaptation
CBDRM	Community-based disaster risk management
CCA	Climate change adaptation
CDA	Collaborative for Development Action
CDKN	Climate and Development Knowledge Network
CDM	Clean Development Mechanism
CEDRA	Climate Change and Environmental Degradation Risk and Adaptation Assessment
COVACA	Community Owned Vulnerability and Capacity Assessment
CRC	[UN] Convention on the Rights of the Child
CRiSTAL	Community-based Risk Screening Tool Adaptations and Livelihoods
CRS	Catholic Relief Services
C-SAFE	Consortium for Southern Africa Food Emergency
CSI	Coping Strategies Index
CSO	Civil society organization
CVCA	Climate Vulnerability and Capacity Analysis
DFID	[United Kingdom] Department for International Development
DMC	Disaster management committee
DRR	Disaster risk reduction
DRRP	Disaster risk reduction plan
ECB	Emergency Capacity Building Project
ECHO	European Commission Directorate General for Humanitarian Aid and Civil Protection
EMI	Earthquakes and Megacities Initiative
EMMA	Emergency Market Mapping Analysis/Assessment
ENF	Earth Net Foundation
ENSO	El Niño Southern Oscillation
FAO	Food and Agriculture Organization of the United Nations
FEG	The Food Economy Group
FMNR	Farmer Managed Natural Regeneration
FUNDEPCO	Fundación para el Desarrollo Participativo Comunitario
GCCA	Global Campaign for Climate Action
GGCA	Global Gender and Climate Alliance
GHG	Greenhouse gases

GIZ	Deutsche Gesellschaft für Internationale Zusammenarbeit
GNDR	Global Network of Civil Society Organisations for Disaster Reduction
GPF	Governance Programming Framework
HEA	Household Economy Approach
HFA	Hyogo Framework for Action
HKSA	Household Livelihood Security Analysis
HVCA	Hazard vulnerability capacity assessment
IDP	Internally displaced persons
IDS	Institute of Development Studies
IEC	Information, Education and Communication materials
IFPRI	International Food Policy Research Institute
IFRC	International Federation of Red Cross and Red Crescent Societies
IIEP	International Institute for Educational Policy
IISD	International Institute for Sustainable Development
ILO	International Labour Organization
INEE	Inter-Agency Network for Education in Emergencies
IPC	Integrated Food Security Phase Classification
IPCC	Intergovernmental Panel on Climate Change
IRI	International Research Institute for Climate and Society
IUCN	The World Conservation Union
IWA	International Water Association
IZA	Institute for the Study of Labor
KAP	Knowledge, Attitudes and Practices survey
LAC	Local Adaptive Capacity framework
LGSAT	Local Government Self-Assessment Tool
LULUCF	Land Use, Land Use Change and Forestry
MEA	Millennium Ecosystem Assessment
MEL	Monitoring, Evaluation and Learning
MIFIRA	Market Information and Food Insecurity Response Analysis
MOSAICC	Modeling System for the Agricultural Impacts of Climate Change
MPBI	Masyarakat Penanggulangan Bencana Indonesia (Indonesian Society for Disaster Management)
NAC	National Adaptive Capacity framework
NAPAs	National Adaptation Programmes of Action
NRM	Natural Resource Management
OFDA	Office of US Foreign Disaster Assistance
ORP	Oral rehydration point
ORS	Oral rehydration solution
PADR	Participatory Assessment of Disaster Risk
PCM	Program Cycle Management
PCVA	Participatory Capacity and Vulnerability Analysis
PDNA	Post-Disaster Needs Assessment
PDNA/RF	Post-Disaster Needs Assessment/Recovery Framework
PECCN	Poverty, Environment and Climate Change Network
PEDRR	Partnership for Environment and Disaster Risk Reduction
PMERL	Participatory Monitoring, Evaluation, Reflection and Learning

RHVP	Regional Hunger and Vulnerability Programme
SDC	Swiss Agency for Development and Cooperation
SEI	Stockholm Environment Institute
SIM	Serving in Mission
SLA	Sustainable Livelihoods Approach
SMART	Specific, Measurable, Achievable, Relevant and Timely
TNA	Training Needs Analysis
UN	United Nations
UNDP	United Nations Development Programme
UNEP	United Nations Environment Programme
UNESCAP	United Nations Economic and Social Commission for Asia and the Pacific
UNESCO	United Nations Educational and Scientific Organization
UNFCCC	United Nations International Conference on Climate Change
UNICEF	United Nations Children's Fund
UNISDR	United Nations International Strategy For Disaster Reduction
UNOCHA	United Nations Office for the Coordination of Humanitarian Affairs
USAID	United States Agency for International Development
VCA	Vulnerability and Capacity Assessment
VS&LA	Village Savings and Loans Associations
WASH	Water, Sanitation and Hygiene
WEDO	Women's Environment and Development Organization
WHO	World Health Organization
WRI	World Resources Institute

Endnotes

1. CRED (2012) `Disaster Data: A Balanced Perspective' CRED CRUNCH Issue 27, Brussels, Belgium: Institute of Health and Society. [Online] www.cred.be/sites/default/files/CredCrunch27.pdf

2. Authors' definition, adapted from UNISDR (2009) *Terminology on Disaster Risk Reduction*. Geneva, Switzerland. [Online] www.unisdr.org/files/7817_UNISDRTerminologyEnglish.pdf

3. Australian Academy of Science (2010) *The Science of Climate Change: Questions and Answers*. Canberra, Australia.

4. Pachauri, R.K. and Reisinger, A. (eds.) (2007) *Climate Change 2007: Synthesis Report*. Contribution of Working Groups I, II and III to the Fourth Assessment Report of the Intergovernmental Panel on Climate Change. Geneva, Switzerland: Intergovernmental Panel on Climate Change.

5. Australian Academy of Science (2010).

6. GNDR (2011) 'If We Do Not Join Hands: Views from the Frontline. Teddington, UK'. [online] www.globalnetwork-dr.org/views-from-the-frontline/voices-from-the-front-line-2011/vfl-2011-final-report-web-version.html

7. UNISDR (n.d.) Briefing Note 03, Strengthening climate change adaptation through effective disaster risk reduction.

8. Pettengell, C. (2010) *Climate Change Adaptation: Enabling people living in poverty to adapt*. Oxford, UK: Oxfam International.

9. While disaster risk reduction and climate change adaptation share common concerns—increased frequency and/or intensity of climate related hazards—disaster risk reduction also deals with non-climate related hazards such as geological and technological hazards.

10. The term 'resilience' is the subject of numerous studies, and its definition is likely to be modified repeatedly in the near future. The definition used in this guide has been adapted from UNISDR (2009) terminology, and DFID (2011) Defining Disaster Resilience: A DFID Approach Paper. London, UK.

11. United Nations (2009) *Global Assessment Report on Disaster Risk Reduction*, Geneva. United Nations (2011) *Global Assessment Report on Disaster Risk Reduction*, Geneva. IPCC (2012) *Special Report of the Intergovernmental Panel on Climate Change: Managing the Risks of Extreme Events and Disasters to Advance Climate Change Adaptation (SREX)*. [Field, C.B.; Barros, V.; Stocker T.F.; Qin, D.; Dokken D.J.; Ebi, K.L.; Mastrandrea, M.D.; Mach, K.J.; Plattner, G.-K.; Allen, S.K.; Tignor, M.: and Midgley, P.M. (eds.)] Cambridge, UK: Cambridge University Press.
    Levine, S.; Ludi, E.; and Jones, L. (2011) *Rethinking Support for Adaptive Capacity to Climate Change: The Role of Development Interventions*, a Report for the Africa Climate Change Resilience Alliance. London, UK: ODI.
    DFID (2011) *Defining Disaster Resilience: A DFID Approach Paper*. London, UK.
    DFID (2010) *Saving lives, preventing suffering and building resilience: The UK Government's Humanitarian Policy*. London, UK.
    Mitchell, T.; Ibrahim, M.; Harris, K.; Hedger, M.; Polack, E.; Ahmed, A.; Hall, N.; Hawrylyshyn, K.; Nightingale, K.; Onyango, M.; Adow, M.; and Sajjad Mohammed, S. (2010), *Climate Smart Disaster Risk Management, Strengthening Climate Resilience*, Brighton, UK, IDS.

12. Case study taken from: Ibrahim M. and Ward N. (2012) *Research Report. Promoting Local Adaptive Capacity: experiences from Africa and Asia*. World Vision UK, UKaid.

13. UNDP (2011) *Social Services for Human Development: Viet Nam Human Development Report 2011*. Hanoi, Vietnam.

14. UNISDR (2001) 'UNISDR says the young are the largest group affected by disasters' [Online] http://www.unisdr.org/archive/22742
15. Seballos, F.; Tanner, T.; Tarazona, M.; and Gallegos, J. (2011) *Children and Disasters: Understanding Impact and Enabling Agency.* Brighton, UK, IDS.
16. Baez, J.; De la Fuente, A.; and Santos, I. (2010) *Do Natural Disasters Affect Human capital? An assessment based on existing empirical evidence.* Discussion paper No. 5164. World Bank and the Institute for the Study of Labor. Available at: http://ftp.iza.org/dp5164.pdf
17. Bartlett, S. (2008) 'The Implications of Climate Change for Children in Lower-Income Countries', *Children, Youth and Environments*, Vol 18. Boulder, Colorado, USA: University of Colorado.
18. Save the Children, Philippines country office 2010.
19. Smyth, I. (2005) 'More than silence: the gender dimension of tsunami fatalities and their consequences'. WHO conference on Health Aspects of the Tsunami Disaster in Asia, Phuket, Thailand.
20. Alson, M. and Kent, J. 'The Big Dry: The link between rural masculinities and poor health outcomes for farming men'. *Australian Journal of Sociology*, June 2008, vol 44, No 2, 133-147.
21. Gautam, D. (2007) 'Floods and need assessment, a sociological study from Banke, Bardiya and Kailali of mid and far-western Nepal', Lutheran World Federation, Nepal, in *We Know What We Need: South Asian women speak out on climate change adaptation*, ActionAid/IDS. Johannesburg, South Africa: ActionAid International.
22. The World Bank and other international organizations use the term 'indigenous peoples' to refer to those with a social and cultural identity distinct from the dominant or mainstream society, which makes them vulnerable to being disadvantaged in development processes.
23. IFAD (2003) *Indigenous Peoples and Sustainable Development Discussion Paper for the Twenty-Fifth Anniversary Session of IFAD's Governing Council*, February 2003.
24. Case study adapted from: Weimer, A. (2008) *Homestead Gardening: A Manual for Program Managers, Implementers, and Practitioners.* CRS. This manual was funded through the FAO as a part of the 2007 Input Trade Fairs project. Additional resources include information from the CRS proposal to OFDA 2011, the project launch interim reports, and from CRS Lesotho staff.
25. Ayers, J.; Anderson, S.; Pradhan, S.; and Rossing, T. (2012) *Participatory Monitoring, Evaluation, Reflection and Learning for Community-based Adaptation: A Manual for Local Practitioners.* Atlanta, USA: CARE International.
26. Ayers et al (2012).
27. These sectors were identified by ECB Project Field Consortium as the key sectors to reference in this guide given that these are the most frequently experienced in their work.
28. FAO (1996) *Rome Declaration and World Food Summit Plan of Action.* [Online] www.fao.org/docrep/003/X8346E/x8346e02.htm#P1_10
29. FAO (2010) *The State of Food Insecurity in the World: Addressing food insecurity in protracted crises.* Rome, Italy. [Online] www.fao.org/docrep/013/i1683e/i1683e.pdf
30. Leather, C. (2009) *Bridging the Divide: The reform of global food security governance.* Oxfam Briefing Note. Oxford, UK: Oxfam International.
31. Beddington J.; Asaduzzaman M.; Clark M.; Fernández A.; Guillou M.; Jahn M.; Erda L.; Mamo T.; Van Bo, N.; Nobre, C.A.; Scholes, R.; Sharma, R.; and Wakhungu, J. (2012) *Achieving food security in the face of climate change: Final report from the Commission on Sustainable Agriculture and Climate Change.* CGIAR Research Program on Climate Change, Agriculture and Food Security (CCAFS). Copenhagen, Denmark: CGIAR.

32. Leather (2009).
33. IPCC (2012) Summary for policy makers. In Field, C.B., et al. (eds.) *Managing the risks of extreme events and disasters to advance climate change adaptation. A special report of Working Groups I and II of the Intergovernmental Panel on Climate Change.* Cambridge, UK: Cambridge University Press. pp 1–19.
34. Beddington et al (2012).
35. IPCC (2012).
36. Oxfam GB (2009) *Disaster Risk Reduction in Livelihoods and Food Security Programming: A Learning Companion.* Oxfam Disaster Risk Reduction and Climate Change Adaptation Resources. Oxford, UK.
37. Beddington et al (2012).
38. Beddington et al (2012).
39. Case study adapted from reports by Francis Dube, Mary Mukwavi, and Gutu Teso of World Vision International.
40. The World Bank (2010) *Ghana: Economics of Adaptation to Climate Change Study* http://climatechange.worldbank.org/content/economics-adaptation-climate -change-study-homepage
41. Pasteur, K. (2011) *From Vulnerability to Resilience: A framework for analysis and action to build community resilience.* Rugby, UK: Practical Action Publishing.
42. Pasteur (2011).
43. Pettengell (2010).
44. IFAD (n.d.) 'The Sustainable Livelihoods Approach'. [Online] http://www.ifad.org/sla/index.htm
45. Quiroga, R. (2009) *Rescuing the Past: Using Indigenous Knowledge to Adapt to Climate Change in Bolivia.* Climate Change Adaptation in Practice case study. Oxfam International. [Online] http://policy-practice.oxfam.org.uk/publications/rescuing-the-past-using-indigenous-knowledge-to-adapt-to-climate-change-in-boli-123849
46. ProAct Network (2008) The Role of Environmental Management and eco-engineering in Disaster Risk Reduction and Climate Change Adaptation. Tannay, Switzerland: ProAct Network. [Online] http://www.unisdr.org/files/4148_emecoengindrrcca1.pdf
47. Pimental, D. (2006) 'Soil Erosion: A Food and Environmental Threat'. *Environment, Development and Sustainability,* Vol 8, No 1, February 2006, pp 119-137.
48. Pimental (2006).
49. FAO (2006) *Global Forest Resources Assessment 2005: Progress towards sustainable forest management.* FAO Forestry Paper 147. Rome, Italy: FAO.
50. OECD (2008) *OECD Environmental Outlook to 2030.* Paris, France: OECD. [Online] www.oecd.org/dataoecd/29/33/40200582.pdf
    Falkenmark, M. and Rockström, J. (2004) *Balancing Water for Humans and Nature. The New Approach in Ecohydrology.*
51. Overexploited: The fishery is being exploited beyond a level believed to be sustainable in the long term.
52. The World Bank (2006) 'The State of the World Fish Stocks'. *Profish Fisheries Factsheet Number 2.* Washington DC, USA.
53. The World Bank (2006).
54. Cassis, G. 1998 'Biodiversity loss: a human health issue'. *The Medical Journal of Australia.* Sydney, Australia: Australasian Medical Publishing Company. [Online] http://210.8.184.99/public/issues/xmas98/cassis/cassis.html
55. Kamara, J.K.; Hailu T.; Toffu, A. (2008). *Humbo Community Managed Natural Regeneration Project PRA Report.* World Vision community re-forestation project in Humbo, Ethiopia: Participatory Rural Appraisal Documentation of Trends. Melbourne, Australia: World Vision Australia.

56. Hagbrink, I. (2010) *Turning it Around: Greening Ethiopia's Great Rift Valley.* Washington DC, USA: The World Bank.

57. Unicef (n.d.) 'Water, sanitation and hygiene' [Online] www.unicef.org/wash/

58. IPCC (2007) Contribution of Working Group II to the Fourth Assessment Report of the Intergovernmental Panel on Climate Change, 2007. [Parry, M.L; Canziani, O.F.; Palutikof, J.P.; Van der Linden, P.J.; and Hanson, C.E. (eds)], Cambridge, UK and New York, NY, USA: Cambridge University Press.

59. Case Study taken from Rottier, Erik (2011) *Risk Returns,* United Nations International Strategy for Disaster Reduction Secretariat (UNISDR), (2011), and CARE Nederland.

60. Right to Education Project, 'Defining the right to education'. Amnesty International, Global Campaign for Education, ActionAid. London, UK. [Online] www.right-to-education.org/node/233

61. A.J. McMichael, A.J.; Campbell-Lendrum, D.H.; Corvalán, C.F.; Ebi, K.L.; Githeko, A.K.; Scheraga, J.D.; Woodward, A. (eds) (2003) *Climate change and human health: risks and responses.* WHO. Geneva, Switzerland.

62. McMichael et al. (2003).

63. WHO (2009) *Protecting health from climate change: Global research priorities.* Geneva, Switzerland.

64. Oxfam GB (2012)

65. Case study adapted from: Fahy, L. (2008) 'Positive and Procedural Obligations Arising from the Right to Life'. *Human Rights Law Centre Bulletin.* No 25 May 2008 pp10-11. [Online] http://www.hrlc.org.au/content/publications-resources/hrlrc-e-bulletin/may-2008/

    Additional material from: Netherlands Institute of Human Rights, Utrecht School of Law (2012) Budayeva and others v. Russia. [Online] http://sim.law.uu.nl/sim/caselaw/Hof.nsf/1d4d0dd240bfee7ec12568490035df05/9d5b59904fdc5060c125740f003 66820?OpenDocument

66. Connolly Carmalt, J. and Haenni Dale, C. (2011) 'Human rights and disaster' in Wisner, B and Gaillard, J.C. and Kelman, I (eds). *The Routledge handbook of hazards and distaster risk reduction.* New York: Routledge.

67. These sectors were identified by ECB Project Field Consortium as the key sectors to reference in the guide given that these are the most frequently experienced in their work.

68. Adapted by the authors from Introduction to the Resource Pack, Conflict Sensitivity. [Online] www.conflictsensitivity.org

69. According to ODI/HPG, between 1999 and 2004 at least 140 disasters happened in contexts that were also experiencing conflict.

70. UNDP (2011) *Disaster-Conflict Interface: Comparative Experiences.* New York, USA: UNDP Bureau for Crisis Prevention and Recovery.

71. Smith, D. and Vivekananda, J., (2007) *A Climate of Conflict: the Links Between Climate Change and War.* International Alert International Alert.

72. Guidance Note on Early Recovery, Cluster Working Group on Early Recovery (2008). Geneva, Switzerland: United Nations Development Program Bureau for Crisis Prevention and Recovery.

73. Case study developed by Martha Kihara, CRS.

74. National Adaptation Programme of Action of the Republic of the Sudan. (2007): Ministry of Environment and Physical Development Higher Council for Environment and Natural Resources, Sudan [online] National Adaptation Programme of Action of the Republic of the Sudan. Khartoum, Sudan (2007): Ministry of Environment and Physical Development Higher Council for Environment and Natural Resources, Sudan.

75. UNOCHA (2011) *OCHA and slow-onset emergencies.* OCHA Occasional Policy Briefing Series No 6. Policy Development and Studies Branch, UNOCHA.

76. Hillier, D. and Dempsey, B. (2012) *A Dangerous delay: The cost of late response to early warnings in the 2011 drought in the Horn of Africa*. Joint Agency Briefing Paper. Oxford, UK: Oxfam International and Save the Children.

77. Hillier and Dempsey (2012).

78. Pachauri, R.K. and Reisinger, A. (eds.) (2007) *Climate Change 2007: Summary for Policymakers*. Contribution of Working Groups I, II and III to the Fourth Assessment Report of the Intergovernmental Panel on Climate, Geneva, Switzerland: IPCC.

79. CARE (2012) *Regional Project for Adaptation to the Impact of Rapid Glacier Retreat in the Tropical Andes – "PRAA", Atlanta, CARE*.

80. Pasteur, K. (2011).

81. GNDR (2011).

82. Pelling, M. (2011) *Adaptation to Climate Change: Resilience to Transformation*. Abingdon, UK: Routledge.

83. Pasteur (2011).

84. Pasteur (2011).

85. Meadowcroft, J. (2010) *Climate Change Governance*. Background paper to the 2010 World Development Report. Policy Research Working Paper 4941. Washington, DC, USA: The World Bank.

86. GNDR (2011).

87. GNDR (2011).

88. Case study prepared by Hening Parlan, Helmi Hamid and Adi Suryadini based on various ECB Indonesia Consortium documents prepared by Hening Parlan, Helmi Hamid and Adi Suryadini.

89. United Nations in Indonesia (2011) *Disaster management: Challenges and opportunities*, http://www.un.or.id/en/what-we-do/partnership-for-development/disaster-management

90. Oktaviani, R.; Amaliah, S.; Ringler, C.; Rosegrant, M.W.; Sulser, T.B. (2011) *The impact of global climate change on the Indonesian economy*. Washington DC, USA: International Food Policy Research Institute, http://www.ifpri.org/publication/impact-global-climate-change-indonesian-economy

91. Willitts-King, B. (independent consultant) *The silver lining of the tsunami?: disaster management in Indonesia; Humanitarian Exchange Magazine*, Issue 43, June 2009. London, UK: Humanitarian Practice Network, Overseas Development Institute http://www.odihpn.org/humanitarian-exchange-magazine/issue-43/the-silver-lining-of-the-tsunami-disaster-management-in-indonesia

92. The Universal Declaration of Human Rights (1948), New York.

93. Project information is available: http://gestionterritorialadaptativa.com/

Index

Contributors

Toward Resilience: A Guide to Disaster Risk Reduction and Climate Change Adaptation was developed through wide-ranging consultations that began in November 2010, through workshops and field tests, and by e-mail and phone discussion. It is based on contributions from the field staff, technical advisors and ECB Project staff of six participating agencies. It has benefited from the expert advice of staff of the Global Network for Disaster Reduction, the UN International Strategy for Disaster Reduction (UNISDR), Feinstein International Center, Worldwide Fund for Nature, Gender and Disaster Network, Humanitarian Futures Program, Plan International, Christian Aid, King's College London, the American Red Cross and other organizations. The Emergency Capacity Building Project gratefully acknowledges the many organizations and individuals who contributed their expertise.

Project host
Catholic Relief Services (CRS)

Project staff
Project Manager: Amy Hilleboe
Publication and launch coordinator: Anne Castleton
Project support: Angela Owen, Angela Previdelli, David Hockaday, Driss Moumane, Gabrielle Fox, LeAnn Hager, Katy Love, Andrea Stewart

ECB DRR Advisor steering committee
Amy Hilleboe, CRS; Anne Castleton, Mercy Corps; Erik Rottier, Care Netherlands; Ian Rodgers and Malka Older, Save the Children; Isabelle Bremaud, Oxfam GB; and Richard Rumsey, World Vision

Editorial committee
Richard Ewbank, Nick Hall, Jim Jarvie, Marcus Oxley, Rod Snider, Peter Walker, Ben Wisner, Emma Visman

ECB Project country consortium representatives
Ade Darmawansyah, Adi Suryadini, Alfonso Ruibal, Ashley Hughes Bishop, Balaram Chandra Tapader, Bijoy Khrishna Nath, Harun Rashid, Helmi Hamid, Idriss Leko, Ingrid Terrazas, Jacklin Ribero, Japheth Mutisya Muli, Luis Alberto Salamanca Mazuelo, Martha Kihara, Massimo Nicoletti Atimari, Omar Saracho, Oyoko Omondo Julius, Roger Quiroga, Shamina Akhtar, Wahyu Widayanto, Zahairu Mamane Sani

Consultants
Authors: Marilise Turnbull and Charlotte L. Sterrett
Editor: Solveig Marina Bang
Translators: Séga Ndoye (French), Patricia Ramos (Spanish)
Translation editors: Elsa Bofill Polsky (French), Rodolfo Valdez (Spanish).

Additional contributors
Chris Anderson, Sophie Blackburn, Christopher Brown, Nyasha Chishakwe, Karl Deering, David R. Dishman, David Dodman, Gillian Dunn, Wynn Flaten, Rachel Houghton, Nick Ireland, Luis Alberto Salamanca Mazuelo, Susan Romanski, Kemi Seesink, Anita Swarup, Suzanna Tkalec, Edward Turvill

Workshop support and field testing
Nancy Wu, Vanessa Wirth, Warinyupha Sangkaew; staff from CRS India, CARE Madagascar, Mercy Corps Nepal, Mercy Corps Tajikistan and World Vision Nicaragua

The Emergency Capacity Building Project

This book is a core resource developed as part of the Emergency Capacity Building (ECB) Project, a collaborative effort by six agencies: CARE International, Catholic Relief Services, Mercy Corps, Oxfam, Save the Children and World Vision International. Working with partners, these agencies are focused on developing joint initiatives to address issues related to national staff development, accountability to disaster-affected people, impact measurement and disaster risk reduction.

The ECB Project goal is to improve the speed, quality, and effectiveness of the humanitarian community to save lives, and to improve the welfare and protect the rights of people in emergency situations. To achieve this goal the ECB Project agencies are working to increase coordination between the humanitarian and development communities, and to enhance coherence between short and longer-term programs.

Bill & Melinda Gates Foundation, the European Commission's Directorate General for Humanitarian Aid & Civil Protection (ECHO), and the Office of US Foreign Disaster Assistance (OFDA) of the United States Agency for International Development (USAID), provided funding for the ECB Project and this book. Fidelity Charitable Trustees' Philanthropy Fund supported the development and publication of this book. We thank them for their generous support.

Notes